"If you've ever wondered what your ⟨ W9-CRM-757 ⟩k is essential reading. Julia Mossbridge is a scientist, but her words speak directly to your soul, the heart and eternal essence of you. Highly recommended."

—**Theresa Cheung**, *Sunday Times* top-ten best-selling spiritual and personal transformation author

"There is a myriad of books published on the subject of finding your purpose. *The Calling* stands out from the rest. It is written by a most superb cognitive neuroscientist using the 'deep scientific method' to lead us in a most exciting prospect: uncovering our callings as we apply the scientific method to ourselves. I highly recommend this book, in which Mossbridge guides us in becoming scientists of our own true work, and takes us inside our own experience, where the truth of our souls is revealed."

—**Justine Willis Toms**, host of *New Dimensions Radio*, coauthor of *True Work*, and author of *Small Pleasures*

"A universal feature of the great spiritual traditions is that there is meaning, purpose, and direction to existence; that happiness and a sense of fulfillment are more likely when one aligns with this felt direction, this calling; and that guides who have 'been there' can assist one's attempts to align with this beckoning from the world. Julia Mossbridge is such a guide, and *The Calling* is her guidebook.

Mossbridge has performed an enormous service, because a characteristic of our age is a widespread experience of ennui, despair, and a sense that what one person does will not matter against the backdrop of seven billion fellow inhabitants of the planet. *The Calling* is an antidote for this world-weariness.

And here's a bonus: Mossbridge is an elite scientist who understands the deep connections between mind and matter, consciousness and the world. She demonstrates why one's calling is not just a personal, individual concern, but is an issue on which the future of our species likely depends. It is difficult to imagine a more urgent concern, or a more valuable (

—Larry I

"Julia Mossbridge has rendered an important service in *The Calling*. She returns us to the origin of the real scientific spirit—the radical idea that the world is knowable. She also moves us into the twenty-first century by giving us a grounding in our own subjectivity, stating boldly that 'the science of your soul's work is to take your inner experience seriously.' Mossbridge gives us new, scientifically based reasons why we should reconsider a cosmology that places us inside the family of interdependent things. If you want to be the person you intuitively know you're capable of being, this book sets out an informed, friendly, and powerful program for getting you there."

—**Rebecca Armstrong, DMin**, mediator, mythologist, cofounder of Mind University, and adjunct faculty in the department of philosophy and religion at Indiana University

"*The Calling* provides a much-needed path to understanding what one was born to do, in a fun-to-read and refreshing alternative to the many self-help books that seek to direct readers toward careers that may or may not be fulfilling (or even the right fit). Through structured, actionable, and sometimes delightfully challenging exercises, Mossbridge deftly guides the reader toward the discovery and celebration of the soul's work—no small task in an era which finds many searching for meaning and purpose."

—**JD Pirtle**, artist, educator, and founder and principal of Depth and Light—an education, design, and technology studio+consultancy based in Chicago, IL

"Julia offers a unique approach to connect more deeply with your authentic self through a scientific process. This playful experiment guides the reader through stages of personal development, which invites clarity, connection, and surrender in pursuing purpose. Sharing stories and providing brief exercises engage the reader with possibilities and practices for getting out of their own way and allowing their soul's calling to emerge. Doing this program with another or in a group may enrich the experiment and outcomes."

—**Maureen Pelton, MSSW, LICSW**, cofounder of ShiftIt Institute, LLC

"Julia Mossbridge has written a must-read guide for anyone who wants to live in alignment with their heartfelt desires. In *The Calling*, she accompanies readers on a twelve-week journey of experimental self-exploration to attain self-knowledge and clarity on what makes their hearts sing. Her voice is clear and compassionate, capturing the essence of all that is truly energizing in our lives and showing that you don't need to sacrifice your passion to live well. Like all things worth doing, the program requires commitment. However, if you truly want to change your life, I cannot recommend this book strongly enough."

—**Isabelle C. Widmer, MD**, life sciences consultant and coach, elytra GmbH

"Ever since I read *The Martian*, I've been trying to 'science' the hell out of my life—nice idea in theory, extremely difficult in execution. With Mossbridge's *The Calling*, we now have the first textbook."

—**Neal H. Patel**, principal product manager at Amazon, founder of Google Human/Social Dynamics, founding member of Google Advanced Technology and Projects, and principal researcher at Google's Project Oxygen

The Calling

A 12-Week
Science-Based Program
to Discover, Energize,
and Engage
Your Soul's Work

JULIA MOSSBRIDGE, PHD

New Harbinger Publications, Inc.

Publisher's Note

Distributed in Canada by Raincoast Books

Copyright © 2019 by Julia A. Mossbridge
Reveal Press
An imprint of New Harbinger Publications, Inc.
5674 Shattuck Avenue
Oakland, CA 94609
www.newharbinger.com

Cover design by Amy Shoup

Acquired by Camille Hayes

Edited by Marisa Solís

All Rights Reserved

Library of Congress Cataloging-in-Publication Data on file

21	20	19								
10	9	8	7	6	5	4	3	2	1	First Printing

For Joseph. May your true work shine!

Contents

Foreword

Our world is becoming increasingly materialistic, with a strong appetite for status, power, possessions, and insatiable dollars in the bank. Amid this drive, what is not always recognized is the yearning that's underneath it all. There is a deep yearning for a sense of peace and stillness, and living aligned with our purpose. Even as we obtain status, power, and more and more material possessions, millions of people still experience high levels of depression, loneliness, anxiety, insecurity, all sorts of fears, and a general sense of "something missing" or "not quite right."

There is something more real that's yet to be fully tapped into in so many of us. This gaping hole has a lot to do with not following our calling—not living on purpose for what we're really here to be.

Material things alone will never bring the fulfillment we each profoundly crave. Having our material needs met, as Julia Mossbridge points out in this book, is certainly a part of uncovering and living our potential. But, as she mentions, those basic needs are just the foundation; material needs alone will never bring the fulfillment we all fundamentally seek and need to live our potential and feel deeply satisfied.

Each of us has a unique gift to offer in being on this planet. We all have a special and particular role to play in the discovery and awakening of consciousness individually as well as collectively. The more aware you are of who you truly are—beyond all the thoughts, ideas, beliefs, and emotions most people identify with—the more you will have the capacity to really see and fully live the unique gifts you're here to give. As Julia writes, "Your calling works almost by itself once you handle the sludge and impediments that are blocking its progress. You can think of your calling as a car that's already been built. You just have to dig it out from under a pile of garbage, activate the engine, clear the road, and go."

Digging out from under all of our "sludge"—our emotional baggage, if you will—is paramount to seeing one's full calling and potential. It's like driving a car with mud all over the windshield. Until you clear the mud from the glass you're looking through, you can't see the boundlessness and fullness of what's inside and outside the car. The same is true for human beings. We can't see or experience our full potential inside or outside without clearing up our sense of self (the lens we look through), which is usually made up of the thoughts and beliefs we hold, the stuck emotions that haven't been allowed to fully be here, our identification with the body, and so on. Inquiring into these long-held beliefs of who we are is the gateway to discovering all of what we're here to do.

Julia does a great job organizing this process of discovering one's calling in three simple—and not necessarily easy—stages: Define your calling. Energize your calling. Engage your calling. She guides readers back home, to one's true essence. As Julia writes, "Your calling is always essentially the same. It is nothing less or more than being who you are so your true work in the world can get done." She takes readers on a journey into authenticity, inner authority, trust, self-love, community, connection, and surrender. These qualities and practices are essential to the development of uncovering and living one's true calling. And although *The Calling* is easy to follow, realistic to work with and implement, and laid out step-by-step, it will invite and involve a real dive into oneself, requiring courage, a curious and open mind, and deep love and compassion for oneself and others.

You are whole. You have all that you need inside of yourself, right now. This is not a process of finding parts of oneself somewhere else and adding them to what you currently take yourself to be. It's a subtraction process—an uncovering or peeling away of that which you think you are—to unmask and awaken all that you truly already are.

The population of this planet is more than seven billion. What would this planet look like with every single person following their calling and living their full purpose and potential? Doing just your part—uncovering all that you truly are—brings fulfillment beyond measure. This fulfillment transcends any fleeting satisfaction gained from material attainment, relationships, power, or status. Realizing who you really are, as infinite awareness, allows limitless space for every aspect of your uniqueness to come forth in full expression.

If we all do our part, and unapologetically be all of who we are, and all of who we're intentionally here to be, we would experience a global shift into more harmony, creative flow, unconditional love, and a vibrant sense of aliveness.

—Carole Griggs, PhD
drcarolegriggs.com

Introduction

Are your needs for general physical health, safety, and human connection basically met?

Are you looking for something else—an understanding of your purpose beyond the basics?

Do you know that you have work to do in the world but you're not quite sure what it is or how to do it?

If you've been tossing around these questions lately, you are probably aware of a desire to do something more satisfying than what you are doing now, even if you have difficulty putting your finger on what exactly that "something more satisfying" is. This "more satisfying" thing is your *calling*. It's your true work. It is what happens when you bring your gifts out into the world and become a part of something greater than yourself.

Insight: Your career, daily work, hobbies, and interests are all likely to change over the course of your life, but your calling is always essentially the same. It is nothing less or more than being who you are so your true work in the world can get done.

Successfully bringing your gifts into the world has been called *self-actualization* by psychologist Abraham Maslow, who also emphasized the importance of *self-transcendence*—joining something larger than yourself to make positive changes in the world. All intelligent and reasonably sane people, as long as they have their basic needs met, have the desire to achieve both self-actualization and self-transcendence. To do both is to pursue your calling.

The order of the steps in the 12-week Calling program, which you will follow in this book, is partially based on Maslow's belief that the desire for self-transcendence arises as a result of beginning to pursue self-actualization (Koltko-Rivera 2006). Most people feel like the desire to self-actualize—to discover, understand, and pursue the purpose of being who they are—comes from the "self" or "soul," which can be thought of as nothing more than a term for the part of us that experiences, from one day to the next, what is happening in our lives. That's why in this book, I sometimes refer to your true work as your "soul's work." The Calling program is intended to help you find out what that is, and pursue it.

About Me and the Origins of the Calling Program

The Calling program originated from my curiosity about what people see as their soul's work in the world. I've asked hundreds of people about their callings, and these conversations have helped them clarify and gain perspective on their true work. A few of these conversations are excerpted to make specific points during the 12 weeks of this program.

The program also has roots in a similar book I wrote in 2002: *Unfolding: The Science of Your Soul's Work*. I lifted a few key stories, exercises, and experiments from that book. But in the past seventeen years I've learned a lot more about what it takes to help people successfully pursue their callings, so this program is built on the feedback and advice I received from *Unfolding*. In addition, experiences from my calling circle—a group of remarkable people with whom I met for more than ten years—were absolutely essential to the development of this program. Finally, some of the writing about authenticity in Week 2 originates from work I did as the science director at Focus@Will Labs, where I learned about how people can use their attention to influence their productivity.

The most important thing that all of these experiences taught me is that the gifts that have made me a productive scientist—observation, curiosity, insight, intuition, and listening—are also very helpful when it comes to understanding how people work. I've drawn on these gifts here, as I teach the deep scientific method to you throughout this book. This is the method that lives as a continuous thread through the program. I'll give you a quick taste of it now, though rest assured you will learn much more as you go through each week's work.

The Deep Scientific Method

Most of us were trained at a young age to think that science is about everything other than *ourselves*. For example, disciplines that study human experience and behavior, such as psychology, anthropology and sociology, are not usually taught prior to college. Meanwhile, physics, chemistry, and biology are taught to middle-schoolers and sometimes even younger children. So our first impressions about what is called "science" don't include the exploration of human nature or human purpose.

Even among neuroscientists, focusing on *subjective experience*—what it feels like to be a human being—is just starting to gain ground. I and most other neuroscientists trained in the 1990s were told that subjective experience was not a useful place to look when trying to understand the brain. In contrast, neuroscientists being trained today are beginning to be taught about the importance of exploring subjective experience in their work.

Similarly, the key to doing the science of your soul's work is to take your inner experience—what goes on inside of you—seriously. Although there has not been a lot of cultural support for taking your own inner space seriously, this program will ask you to do so. The reason this is so important is that you will only be able to hear clues to your calling in your inner space. They don't come from anywhere else. So without taking that space seriously, you won't be able to listen.

Insight: You can apply the scientific method to whatever you want, including yourself.

Most of us have been taught that the scientific method is a relatively boring set of steps that we should memorize and maybe try to use the night before we have to turn in our lab notebooks for some high school chemistry or biology course. Develop a hypothesis, test it by running an experiment, observe the data and form conclusions, and try to write down what we think the teacher wants to hear.

This version of the method is remarkably powerful, of course. But it's not the *heart* of the scientific method in its original form. It's not what I call the *deep scientific method*, which I believe is used by virtually every scientist who actually does experiments and creates models. The deep scientific method is way more fun and way more powerful. It's based on the idea that what scientists do is discover and learn to understand processes, not things. In other words, scientists are always studying change, and trying to understand change.

The deep scientific method goes like this:

Define a process you're interested in,

Energize the process by building a model of it, and

Engage the process and watch it change the world.

The deep scientific method is magical. It is play with a purpose. This kind of play doesn't just help us harness chemical transitions, predict astronomical events, and cure medical conditions. It can also be applied to the processes we are focused on here: self-actualization and self-transcendence.

To really engage the Calling program, you'll need to become the scientist of your own true work. That means you'll need a lab notebook. This is where you'll record the results of every experiment and brief exercise during the next 12 weeks. Without your lab notebook, you won't be able to do the work in the program, so get one before you start your first experiment in Week 1.

How the Calling Program Works

In this program, you're the scientist, and the process you're investigating is your calling. The first four weeks are about defining your calling so that you have a clear idea about what it is. The second four weeks are about energizing your calling by doing the work it takes to build a detailed user's guide for yourself. The final four weeks focus on engaging your calling in the world in a playful way, which you can continue to do for the rest of your life.

There is a clear assumption in this program, and I think it's a good one: *Your calling works almost by itself once you handle the sludge and impediments that are blocking its progress.* You can think of your calling as a car that's already been built. You just have to dig it out from under a pile of garbage, activate the engine, clear the road, and go. That's what this program does for you, in a step-by-step fashion. The work is simple: you read stories, explanations, and insights; do brief exercises; and complete at least one experiment per week for 12 weeks.

This program is meant to be completed in 12 continuous weeks, but it's not necessary to finish it in that time frame. If a certain week takes more than seven days to complete, that's okay. A "week" is really however long it takes to get through a chapter.

Having said that, consider trying to finish each chapter in a week. Especially for scientist-types, it's easy to get hung up on making sure that your work each week is completely perfect. Challenge yourself to read the words and do all the exercises and experiments within a week, and consider that week done once you do these things. The program builds on itself, so if you don't get something exactly right the first time, another layer of the same idea or skill will come along soon enough, and you'll get it the second or third time.

Myths About Your Calling

Before we begin with the first week, let's explore some common myths about what your calling is or has to be. This will help you recognize where your misconceptions might be before you begin trying to define your calling.

The myth of *perfection*. Many of us have been told that our calling is God-given or divine. To some of us, this means that our true work has to be perfect at all times. The problem with this is that we know we're not perfect! This puts us in a doomed position: we must do this perfect thing with our imperfect selves. It's worth being curious about whether some part of you believes that you have to be perfect. If so, that's fine, this program should help cure you of that belief. Just know for now that your calling will not be perfect nor should it be. It's a process—it will evolve.

The myth of *responsibility*. You might think you are responsible for your calling, and you're right—sort of. You're responsible for pursuing your calling. But you do not have responsibility for *what* your calling is. You don't choose your calling, just like you don't choose your eye color. Both are embedded in who you are. No one can say whether your calling is mostly genetic, given by life experience, or offered to you as some kind of spiritual process—and it doesn't really matter. The critical point is that you consider the idea that you don't choose your calling; it is just part of who you are. Take a moment to notice whether you believe the myth that you are responsible for what your calling is. If so, please know that this sense of responsibility will be lifted from your shoulders.

The myth of *justification*. This is the idea that if it weren't for your true work, you would have no reason to be here. In other words, it's the erroneous belief that your calling justifies your life. If you feel this way, consider instead that your calling is a description of what you love to do while you are alive. Sometimes you will be doing it, sometimes you won't. But at all times you deserve to be alive. I'll say this again, because it's crucially important. Your calling does not justify your existence. You don't *have* to define, energize, and engage your calling. You *want* to.

Insight: Your calling does not justify your existence; you need no justification to exist.

Every one of us has a calling that is unique, possible, life giving, and important. In a way, your calling is simple: it is to do what you do when you are living as who you are. We all share this generic calling. Your unique calling can be found in the all-important details, which we're going to work out now. Let's begin.

PART I

Discover Your Calling

I magine that your future self has a message for you every day, and each day your job is to receive it and do what is needed to move closer to your future self. How can you learn to listen to this relatively quiet and potentially confusing "call"?

The next four weeks will be a crash course in learning how to listen for your calling and how to really hear the meaning behind it. For many years, scientists learn how to design experiments that almost surreptitiously get nature to reveal its mysteries; they also learn how to interpret the results that arise from these experiments. In graduate school, during postdoctoral work, and throughout early career years, they are continually learning to wade through complex data and multiple unknowns to get a clearer sense of what nature is telling them—just as you'll do with data from your own life in the process of finding your calling.

Fortunately, the process will be expedited here. In the coming four weeks, you will work through the graduate school portion of this program, with the goal of really defining your true work. After that, the following four weeks will be like the postdoctoral years of deepening understanding and energizing your focus, and the final weeks will be analogous to a scientist's early career time, in which you figure out how to engage your passion in the real world.

Assuming you already have your lab notebook, it's time for your first task: preparing your inner laboratory!

Preparing Your Inner Laboratory

Objective: To use your intuition and your fears to prepare an inner space, called your *inner laboratory*, a safe place to listen for clues to your calling.

Welcome to Your Inner Lab!

This first week, you will take upon yourself the responsibility of setting up your own inner space—in this program, this is called your *inner laboratory*. This will be your listening station for clues to your calling. The reason you're reading this book and working through this program is that you want to know your calling, so you need to get into a receptive mode to learn something new about yourself. To get into that mode and make conditions right for insight, you will do what every scientist-in-training does before trying to learn something new: you will arrange things inside yourself so that you can best hear the clues that nature will give you.

There are two steps to preparing your inner lab:

1. Learning to use intuition

2. Becoming well acquainted with your fears

We'll start with your intuition.

Intuition

Your intuition—including your hunches, senses, and gut feelings—knows what you need to feel safe. You'll find that in many of the exercises and experiments in this program, again and again, you are asked to "enter your inner lab." But if your inner lab doesn't feel safe, you won't spend much time there. Making your inner lab a safe, comfortable, and inviting place to be is essential to each of the three parts of this program. So let's get to the work of listening to your intuition!

Wait, why would this be work? If intuition is a natural part of our minds, why would we have to work on listening to it? If you're like most people, the answer is that something gets in the way of listening to your intuition. What could that be?

Here are some possibilities: First, you might contrast intuition with reasoning ability, and you might feel that if you boost your intuition, your reasoning will fail. If so, rest assured that reason is considered an important contributor to good intuition (Baylor 1997). Second, because you believe you can trace your own logic, you might balk at an answer from your intuition that comes out of the blue. However, this reasoning itself doesn't stand up to science. Our conscious minds can serially process up to four factors and come to reasonable decisions based on these factors. Meanwhile, nonconscious intuition works as a parallel process, is available to process many more than four factors at once, and gives us insight into complex problems (Dijksterhuis et al. 2003, Hassin 2013).

Life choices are complex problems with more than four factors in almost every case. For example, each of your life decisions may affect two parents, several children, one or two friends, and five or so coworkers. And that's just people—what about financial, ecological, and social or cultural impacts of our decisions? Given this level of complexity, would you rather trust a linear, serial-processing system that maxes out at four factors but at least allows you to follow its logic, or a nonlinear, parallel-processing system that routinely deals with multiple factors and presents its results to the conscious mind without an explanation? The correct response, if you care more about getting a useful answer than about your need to understand how you got it, is to learn to trust your intuition.

Good scientists must develop and listen to their intuitions about the types of problems they are working on. Figuring out your calling is no different. Having said that, it's important to recognize that intuitions won't always solve your problem. Often your intuition just reveals the next step.

Also, especially when you first start engaging your intuitive abilities, the strength of a particular intuition has no relationship to the accuracy of that intuition. Therefore, ignore the strength and count all intuitions as equal—at first. This does not pose a risk to you of trusting the "wrong" information. The correctness of an intuition is always tested in the real world by doing an experiment. In this program, you'll test your intuitions by doing experiments on yourself.

> **Insight:** Just because you have a strong intuition doesn't mean it is right. Conversely, if you only have a weak intuition, that doesn't mean it's wrong.

If you're like most of us, you have been trained for many years to reason, but your intuitive abilities were left to develop on their own. So we're going to help your intuition draw on your reasoning abilities by using an experiment to connect your reasoning abilities with intuitive insights about your inner lab.

⚗ Saying Yes to Your Inner Lab

Goal: To gather a few preliminary intuitions about your inner lab and record your observations when you are done.

Time required: 15–20 minutes

As you do this experiment, keep in mind that you really can't do it wrong, because the point is to say yes to everything you think and feel about your inner lab, and to notice what those thoughts and feelings are.

1. Prepare.

   Set a five-minute timer and make an overarching intention to tune in to your intuitions about what you need in your inner lab.

2. Say yes to your body's wisdom.

   Ask your body what it needs in your inner lab to feel safe and supported. Feel your whole body—everything. Feel the parts that are sore and the parts that are relaxed and free. Cuticles and nose hairs are not off-limits! As you feel each part, don't try to change it. Instead, just say yes to yourself or even aloud.

3. Say yes to your mind's wisdom.

   Ask your mind what it needs in your inner lab to feel safe and supported. When thoughts, ideas, or feelings about your inner lab come up, don't try to name them or change them. Just say yes. As you say yes to an idea or thought, know that this does not necessarily mean you agree with it. For example, if you have a thought that you want your inner lab to have plush carpeting and wood paneling, you can say yes to it—as in, "Yes, there is a part of me that really wants plush carpeting and paneling on the walls of my inner lab." But you don't need to act on any desires, images, or thoughts right now. If the timer dings and you are not yet done, keep going.

4. Record your observations.

   Write your observations in your lab notebook. What thoughts and feelings did you discover? Does your intuition tell you what these thoughts and feelings might reveal about what your inner lab looks and feels like?

5. Listen to your intuition.

   Set a second overarching intention to listen to your intuition in a way that's both easy and fun. Take a moment to ask your intuition a few questions you might want to know about your inner lab, and listen carefully to any answers that appear. It is a good idea to ask where you'll "put" your laboratory—is it located in a part of your body? Or outside of it? Is it in a beautiful garden in your mind? A private cottage out back? Does your lab show up when you close your eyes or when you go into your office or when you say a certain phrase? Is there anything you can do physically to get yourself situated in your inner lab? What about getting out of it? Any other questions? You don't have to receive any answers at all, and if you do get some answers, you don't have to be certain of them to go on to the next step.

6. Try entering your inner lab.

   You have used your intuition to get some good ideas about your inner lab; now it's time to determine if you can access your inner lab and see what it's like. Set a timer for another five minutes.

7. Observe your experience.

   Now set a third overarching intention to test out your inner lab. See the location of your inner lab—as shown to you by your intuition or wherever your inner lab "appears" now. Do you like it there? If not, move it someplace that feels better. Enter your inner lab in the way your intuition showed you or in the way that is just happening right now. Did it work? If not, try another way to gain entry.

   Once in your lab, check out its decorations (if any), hear its sounds, meet the people there (if any), look at what's around you (furniture, plants, equipment). Ask yourself if you want to change anything. If you do, change it. Once you feel that you absolutely love it, and you feel safe, go ahead and try to leave your inner lab. If whatever you try doesn't work, try something else.

8. Record your results.

   Now that you've tested out your inner lab space, write down in your lab notebook what you learned about your inner lab. You can come and go whenever you like, and you can remain in there for as long as you want.

Congratulations! You've worked with your intuition to make a beautiful space for discovering and defining your calling. Your inner lab will probably change over time, depending on what you need. You can always return to this first experiment at any point throughout this program to redefine what your inner lab looks and feels like, and how you can get into and out of it.

You're well on your way to being able to use this essential inner space to help define your calling. You have one final step: working with the fears that could keep you from really utilizing your inner lab.

Fears

Fear is the number-one block to being able to really use your inner lab. You may have already noticed some fears creeping in during the first experiment you did. You might have felt some resistance to setting up your lab or listening to your intuition completely. When embarking on this type of work, people commonly have worries such as: "Everyone has a calling except me" or "Finding my calling is frivolous or only for privileged folks" or "Life has no meaning, so the idea of a calling isn't rational."

In its most mundane and insidious manifestation, fear can block your ability to move forward by making you feel that you have better things to do. That feeling that you have something better to do than find your calling is a lie—even those with very few resources and many better things to do can discover their callings. Daryl is a good example.

Daryl: A Calling to Heal

I met Daryl* outside a bookstore in Evanston, Illinois, where he was charging his cell phone—one of his few possessions. He was in his thirties and homeless when I interviewed him. His father had died when he was eighteen months old, and his *mother became mentally ill as a result of the stress. She developed an identity disorder, and while one of her "personalities" was maternal toward Daryl, the other was cruel. Daryl's older brother beat him, and at one point his mother shot her oldest son to protect Daryl. His brother survived, but Daryl was negatively impacted by the stress of all he had witnessed and felt, leading to thoughts of suicide and eventual homelessness.*

Daryl was also positively impacted by events in his life, such as when someone brought him to a natural healer when he was suicidal. This healer taught him about herbs, visualizations, and his inner self; she told him he had a calling to heal himself and others. She worked with Daryl to help him move beyond his fears. As a result of studying with her, moving past his fears, and using his wide-ranging intelligence, Daryl says his approach to people has become kinder and more focused on healing.

Although his mother is sick with Alzheimer's and still mentally ill, he thinks well of her and does what he can to help. Each morning he wakes up with the sunrise, walks to the lake, and takes beautiful photos for his daily social media post. I asked him why he does this small act each day, and he says it gives him joy to know that the beauty of the world can be transmitted, via his photos, to heal others. It's clear that Daryl has embraced the twists and turns of his life path. When I asked him what he would tell his younger self at eighteen months old, after his father died, he said, "Be patient. Don't change. Remain yourself."

Use Daryl's story to speak directly to anything in yourself that makes you think that you have better things to do than discover your calling. If Daryl can pursue his calling with his phone and his big heart, there is no question that you can too. This brief exercise will help you blast through any blocks your fears might be putting up.

Brief Exercise

Let's get to the bottom of what it is you might be afraid of when it comes to discovering and defining your calling.

1. Go into your inner lab.

2. Write down the following common fears in your lab notebook:

   - I don't have true work.

   - My true work isn't unique.

   - My true work isn't good.

   - My true work is too big.

   - My true work is too small.

   - I won't be able to do my true work.

   - My true work will change my life in a way I don't want.

3. Write down two of your own fears.

4. Circle your top three fears.

What are your top three fears? Once you have a sense of them, it's time to put them in the mirror. In other words, it's time to examine your *mirror fears*.

Insight: When you are aware of a fear about something, you are often unaware that you have a deeper fear of its opposite.

Fran Townsend, former homeland security adviser to President George W. Bush, revealed her mirror fear when she described her experience reporting for her first day of work at the White House (Politico 2017). As she drove to work, she was afraid they wouldn't have her name on the list to get through the gates. But when she saw in her rear-view mirror the gates close behind her, anxiety overtook her and she found herself thinking, "Oh my God, I got in! What if I can't do it?"

Townsend's initial fear was that they wouldn't have her name on the entry list. But her deeper fear—her mirror fear—was that they would, and that she couldn't do the very difficult job. She was only aware of her deeper fear once she literally looked in the mirror and realized her first fear was unfounded. Such mirror fears aren't always deeper and more profound than the fear we already know about, but surprisingly often they turn out to be.

Brief Exercise

Now it's time to look at your mirror fears about your calling.

1. Now that you've selected your top three fears about defining your true work, let's reverse them and see what your mirror fears might be. For instance, if you chose "I don't have true work" as one of your fears, the mirror version would be "I do have true work." Would that scare you, if you discovered you actually have true work? Another example: If you chose "My true work will change my life in a way I don't want," the mirror fear would be "My true work will change my life in a way I do want." What if your life got better as a result of pursuing your calling? In what ways could that be terrifying?

2. Allow yourself to experience your mirror fear without doing anything about it. Just sit with it and see what happens. Notice that the idea is to ask yourself to describe your feelings—not why you have them.

3. Once you are done, record what you learned in your lab notebook.

There's a lot of misinformation about fear in the world. Many people think that if you say your fears out loud, your fears will dominate you. The reasoning is that if you admit you're afraid, the fear will take over. But instead, the data show that if you can observe your fear or other uncomfortable feelings from the outside (a fly-on-the-wall view), you can feel these feelings and learn something from them without being dominated by them. In fact, people who do this *self-distancing* practice feel better, not worse, after they do it (e.g., Kross and Ayduk 2011).

When I worked with students who had math anxiety, I would tell them to split their math notebooks into halves. One half was for working on the homework problems, while the other half was for their feelings—they could write "I am afraid I'll never learn this" or "I'm too stupid for math" or "I actually like this; does that mean I'm abnormal?" Once they wrote these feelings down, the feelings were less likely to dominate them, not more. Most of the students felt freed up and better able to work the problems after writing their feelings down.

As a scientist, you first need to have experiences close up, then get a bit of separation from them. So first you might say, "I'm terrified that…" or "I'm afraid that…" For example, "I'm afraid that I won't be able to do my true work." Once you really feel the fear, then you could try rephrasing it to say, "I am aware of a fear that I won't be able to do my true work." Feeling the fear intimately and then at a distance are both important, but once you can get a bit of separation from any uncomfortable emotion, you can be curious. Curiosity leads to excitement, which is the first step in the *deep scientific method* as described in the introduction.

Insight: A useful way to manage any uncomfortable feeling is to feel it fully, then observe it from a distance and get curious about it.

What does all this have to do with the inner lab, again? The tools required to make your inner lab a safe, comfortable space for you to discover and define your calling are: accessing your intuition and working skillfully with your fears. To complete the preparations of your unique inner lab space, spend a moment with the final exercise for this week:

Brief Exercise

Use your fears to rework your inner lab.

1. Take a moment and look back at your top three fears and their mirror fears from the previous exercise.

1. For just for a moment, feel each fear closely, then at a distance. Keep it short—don't overthink this.

2. Now read the description of your inner lab that you created in the Saying Yes to Your Inner Lab experiment. Read every word out loud. Does each word still feel right to you now that you've worked with your fears? Is anything missing from your lab to help you feel safe? If so, write down what's missing and correct the description of your inner lab. Keep going until the description is perfect for your needs right now, with the knowledge that it could change even as soon as tomorrow or next week.

You're getting in the habit of using your fears—and other uncomfortable feelings—to do the science of your true work. You'll do this all along in this program, and it will get easier and more effortless each time.

Conclusion

Your inner lab—the space inside of you that no one else can access—is a haven for this work of defining, energizing, and engaging your calling. For most of us, this space was previously ignored, as we spent our time continually responding and reacting to the exterior world and not attending to what was inside.

Setting up your inner laboratory and exploring fears and uncomfortable feelings about your calling is the prerequisite for next week's work. The coming week will be work-heavy and intensive—but well worth it. You'll explore your authentic self, a gem that begins to emerge when you clean off the sludge that's been layered on by everyday attempts to feel okay in this often-difficult world.

WEEK 2

Experimenting with Authenticity

Objective: To gather important clues about your calling by connecting with your authentic self and deepening your relationship with your superconscious.

What Is Authenticity?

One assumption of this program is that some part of you knows what your soul's work is. Sometimes you have insights and brief flashes of your calling when your conscious mind glimpses what's otherwise buried. But because of the way the world works, your inclinations, passions, and knowledge about your true work are probably covered up with something like sludge. The sludge can be due to disappointment, wanting to please others, not wanting to hope, a fear of failure, or any number of things. It doesn't matter right now. What matters right now is learning to be in an authentic state as much as possible. This practice helps remove sludge so that your calling can shine. It'll take some doing, so this week's work is more intense than most. Take heart—by the end of this week, you'll have your first set of clues to help you define your calling.

In this program, *authenticity* is defined as *the state of being aware of and connected to what is true for you in this moment.* Your *authentic self* is who you are when you are in that state. For instance, if what is true for you in this moment is that you're exhausted and overwhelmed, if you are aware of that experience and you accept that the experience is happening, then you are in an authentic state. On the other hand, you are in an inauthentic state if you are either: (1) unaware of your feelings of exhaustion and overwhelm, or (2) trying to distance yourself from the truth of your exhaustion and overwhelm, for example, by trying to appear to have it all together. (Not that any of us would ever do that!)

When you're in an authentic state, it is much easier to discover what is important to you. Also, in an authentic state, you have a greater capacity to remember these discoveries, even if you might not at a given moment have the ability to act on them.

Stephen: A Flickering Light

Stephen*, a colleague of mine who was in his fifties when I interviewed him, is a successful researcher, author, and professor. He currently studies human development and specializes in understanding self-actualization and happiness. In the process of telling me about his calling and how he grew to understand and pursue it in the world, I asked him about his early struggles related to accessing his authentic self.

Stephen told me that his parents and the culture in which he was raised had communicated to him that the only path in life in which someone can be successful is as a business executive. In his twenties, he was working in a coveted position in finance in a big city, following the proscribed path. But one evening, he had a reckoning. He remembered sitting on his mattress in his apartment and reaching for some academic journals he had purchased. As he began to read, his mind was drawn into deep curiosity about the larger world, a curiosity he recognized that he had always had, ever since he was a child. Then a thought entered his head: "If I don't act on the passion that draws me to this larger world, the light inside of me will flicker out, leaving my life empty." He knew he had to find a way to depart from the proscribed business-executive path, but Stephen wasn't sure how, because he felt trapped in the need for approval from family and friends.

Stephen tried several times to break away from his original conditioning, only to find himself attempting to regain approval from his family and to get back into business. But each time he slid back to that place of approval-seeking, he caught a glimpse of that flickering light and the epiphanic moment on his mattress when he had experienced being authentically connected to himself. These repeated experiences eventually caused him to enroll in a PhD program at a major university to study human development. This decision transformed the relationship Stephen had with work; he became immersed in what he says was the deepest and most satisfying meditation of his life: a fourteen-year study in which he set out to discover what drives people to do work and what makes them feel whole.

How did Stephen repeatedly sense the flickering light of his passion? He did it by being authentically connected to himself. Informed by Stephen's story of letting himself use this light as a touchstone, let's first examine what happens when we're not authentically connected to ourselves.

The Perils of Inauthenticity

How many of us have wanted to evoke a particular reaction in someone else—for instance, to make a good impression—and, as a result, we fell out of an authentic state? In these moments, instead of staying connected to yourself and hoping someone will be impressed with who you actually are, you disconnected from yourself to evoke a hoped-for response. Funny thing is, on the rare occasions when the other person was actually impressed with this show, you found you didn't care as much as you thought you would, because you secretly knew you weren't being yourself! The other person was impressed with a false self, so even if you felt good for a short time, you inevitably realized that their approval didn't really count.

> **Insight:** Inauthenticity usually happens as a result of trying to seek some wished-for outcome. But if you get the outcome you seek, you're not connected with yourself enough to enjoy it.

Think of a moment when you have done this. For instance, maybe you were really annoyed with your boss, but you decided to compliment your boss about the very thing that annoyed you. To speak that compliment (which was essentially a lie), you had to distance yourself from your own experience. That distancing feeling is a telltale sign of inauthenticity, and it feels crappy.

To make matters worse, other people often know when you're not being real, and no one likes it. For instance, fake smiles are not only easy to detect as fakes, they evoke less pleasure than real smiles in the person who sees them (Frank, Ekman, and Friesen 1993; Surakka and Hietanen 1998). These habitual types of false-self responses are actually clues that we're in an inauthentic state. Almost everyone uses them, and most people can see right through them.

But you're a scientist here, and in this part of the work you have a goal: to get a clear definition of your calling. In order to do that, you have to work with the material you have to connect with your authentic self. What material do you have? One thing that is probably abounding in your life, if you're a human in the twenty-first century, is the *inauthentic habit* of checking in with your technological devices for no reason other than to avoid feeling your feelings. Here, an inauthentic habit is one that shows you that you are not in an authentic state.

Luckily, it turns out that inauthentic habits can be great raw material for getting into an authentic state. Whenever you notice one in yourself, you can remind yourself to go into your inner lab—to check in with your own inner experience—and accept your actual feelings and thoughts, in that moment. Not the judgments you have about those thoughts or the concerns you have about how your feelings might be inappropriate, annoying, or wrong, but the actual thoughts and feelings themselves.

Brief Exercise

Every time you check your cell phone or email, or make another habitual move during the day, do a quick check for your authenticity.

1. Ask yourself, "What is my inner experience right now?" Listen for the answer.

2. Love the answer itself, no matter what it is.

3. Love yourself for having the answer, no matter what it is. If you are aware of your inner experience and you are connected to that inner experience, you are in an authentic state—even if that inner experience is "I wonder what my inner experience is?"

If you found yourself struggling with this exercise, keep in mind that there's a whole perfectionism thing that happens in the personal growth/mindfulness/meditation world. Unfortunately, it can feed inauthenticity. We can feel as if we are supposed to have only positive thoughts and feelings, as if we're supposed to have a blank mind, or as if we're supposed to be filled with compassion for the world. These restrictions on what can be true for us end up driving our actual inner experience underground. We worry that our thoughts and feelings are not kind enough, not perfect enough. Well, how many times have I personally realized that my inner experience was that I wanted to throttle someone? I can't count them! But the power is not in placing some kind of judgment over those experiences. It's in experiencing them and appreciating them for what they are: feelings and thoughts. So doing, it's easier to let them go and move on.

Want more motivation to practice authenticity? People who report that they feel authentic also have objectively greater well-being and psychological adjustment (Kernis 2003). And several workplace studies show that team leaders and work groups who spend most of their work time in an authentic state are more productive (Hannah, Walumbwa, and Fry 2011; Walumbwa et al. 2008). But for your work now, authenticity matters because access to information about your calling blossoms when you are authentic and wilts when you are inauthentic. The more you practice checking in with and loving what is true for you right now, the more often you will be in an authentic state and the more correct information you will learn about your calling.

Authenticity Needs Only a Little Nudge

Letting yourself be in an authentic state is addictive and requires only a little outside support, once it is allowed at all. Even in a hostile environment that exerts pressure on you to be inauthentic, if you get some kind of positive response from one other person, you can increase the time you spend in an authentic state. Here's a personal example:

I was raised in a family that oozed unpredictability. Intense rages dominated one minute, lengthy discussions of raw feelings permeated the next. Mental illness in my parents resulted in mild abuse and trauma for me and my sister. Like many people exposed to this environment, I wanted nothing more than to control my experience. I tried to represent myself in certain ways so that I could reliably get approval from others. It didn't work, but I tried hard. Being a successful student with no obvious emotional needs—that was how I wanted to be seen by others, both inside and outside of my family. As a result, during my childhood, I spent a decent amount of time in an inauthentic state.

But here's the paradox: despite this mess of pain and suffering, and despite my attempts to control the mess through manipulation of others and misrepresentation of myself, my parents somehow supported my authenticity on the occasions when it showed up. This, despite the same parents seemingly wishing for me to act from a false self who had no need for them. I distinctly remember a moment in which my stepmom told me that she really loved having conversations with me when I was just being myself.

A light bulb turned on. I thought, "Wait, other people can tell when I'm being myself, *and they like it?*" And true enough, I found that when I told my parents unpleasant things that were nonetheless true for me, such as how pissed I was about the abuse, they listened. And they continue to do so. Even now into their eighties, they seem to be able to tolerate me being aware of and connected to my feelings, and they are proud of me when I can achieve that awareness and connection as I go about my professional life. I know this is rare. Very few people who seemed to require inauthenticity to manage mentally ill parents also had, from these same parents, major explicit support for their authenticity.

But that's why I'm telling this story—to reveal the power provided by just a little support, even when that support comes from an environment that is simultaneously hostile to authenticity. The way I see it, despite the obvious paradoxes in my family, this clear support for authenticity fed my ability to be courageous in many ways.

It's worth asking yourself what *your* life experience has taught you about authenticity. What factors might make it difficult for you to become aware of and connected to what is true for you right now? Were there folks in your life who encouraged you to be exactly who you are? Or were these people absent altogether?

Support is critical. First, without support for your authenticity, sludge covers up your calling, so you can't see it. Second, when you have support for your authenticity, you can overcome almost anything. That's because you're being told that who you are is actually more than okay—it's preferable compared to who you are not. So even if no one else supports you being in an authentic state, for now please think of me as support for your authenticity, regardless of your environment. In the second part of the program, we'll get you a support circle.

Inner Experience versus Outer Actions

People who seem hostile to your attempts at being who you are aren't the only barriers to authenticity. There are rules about what is appropriate and what is not appropriate to say and do, and if you violate these rules, you risk becoming isolated and lonely. If you interpret authenticity as saying and doing only what you feel like saying and doing, then it really does seem that these rules about appropriate actions will keep you from experiencing your authenticity.

However, without saying or doing anything about your inner experience, it turns out that you can be aware of what is true (example: "I feel like quitting my job, right now!") and connected to it as well (example: "It's okay that I feel like quitting my job, and I wonder what that is telling me?"). The point is, you are in an authentic state if you are aware of and engaged with what is true for you, regardless of what you choose to say or do about it.

> **Insight:** Acknowledging and loving your inner experience is safe, kind, and will move you forward. Acting on your inner experience may or may not be any of these things.

The division between internal experience (which we are all free to have) and the external expressions of those experiences (which have some societal constraints) has not been made so clearly for most of us. What often happens is that people believe that their thoughts and feelings are inappropriate. Then they try to not feel these thoughts and feelings by either ignoring them or harshly judging them. The work here is to notice if you are doing this, and then go back to being in an authentic state by accepting your thoughts and feelings without assuming you have to act on them. Only then are you in a better state to try to figure out what action would be best in that moment, including waiting until you have greater clarity.

But remember, the reason we're delving into day-to-day authenticity is that it is a key tool for sorting out the clues to your calling. You'll have to be in an authentic state to get those clues. One helper tool for testing whether an idea, feeling, thought, or situation is authentically connected to your calling is what I call your *truth reaction*—the physical feeling you get when something is right for you. Having this truth reaction can even involuntarily put you in an authentic state!

What's Your Truth Reaction?

I have a friend who returned from a trip to Boston glowing with exciting stories. She had fallen in love with her thighs, met a wonderful woman, and slept in satin sheets. One of her stories was about an experience she had sitting beneath a tree and thinking about her life. She said that when she happened upon a deep truth, she knew it was true because her whole body tingled; she felt like she was a bell vibrating with the "ring" of truth.

This story stuck with me, and I began to experiment with my physical response to truth. I found that when I think, feel, read, or hear about something that is crucial to my true work, the hair on the back of my neck stands on end. Other people experience tingling, get goose bumps, or feel "fluttery." It turns out that these physical reactions to truth are very common. Right now, you might have a sense of yours, or you might only be aware of thoughts related to truth but not physical feelings. A physical truth reaction is a lot more direct than a mental one, so yours is worth finding. If you don't know what your truth reaction is, this experiment will help you find it.

♨ The Truth Experiment

Goal: To use your truth reaction to practice connecting authentically with clues about your calling.

Time required: 15–20 minutes

This is about telling the radical truth, the truth at the root of your feelings. This experiment does not ask you to tell the deep-down truths that might hurt people's feelings or damage relationships. It asks you to tell the even deeper-down truths that really alter the way you live in the world. Radical truth telling supports authenticity. If you practice radical truth telling, you will find that you and your friends, family, and partner discover who you really are, and you learn more about your calling.

1. Notice when you don't feel like yourself.

    Enter your inner lab and bring to mind a moment in the past in which you didn't feel like yourself—something that could happen again. For example, maybe you're aware that you didn't feel like yourself when Stephanie walked into the conference room at work. Recall the moment of inauthenticity. Go into your inner lab with the intention of taking a curious look at this experience.

2. Notice your deeper experience.

    By taking a curious look at your experience, you may notice something that underlies it. Ask yourself what conflict there might have been for you in the situation. You might also notice something that got in the way of clearing the conflict at the moment it occurred. For example, by curiously noticing your memory of your reaction when Stephanie walked into the room, you discover that you have a little crush on her. The conflict is that Stephanie is your coworker and you rightly feel it would be inappropriate to tell her about your crush.

3. Find the deepest truth for you.

    Dig even deeper. What truth underlies this truth? Keep digging. You know when you have gotten deep enough when the truth is about your feelings and not someone else's behavior, when the truth is not likely to harm you or someone else, and when it causes a physical feeling that comes over you—that's your truth reaction. Once you discover the deepest truth, spend a moment receiving it in your body. Say it out loud and let yourself respond to it. Keep saying it until it becomes a fact, rather than a threat.

For example, you discover that you admire people who have a lot of power, and Stephanie is one of those people. By noticing your truth reaction, you realize that you are attracted to these people because you want more power in your life. Saying to yourself, "I want more power in my life" makes you have your truth reaction, even though it might also make you cringe. Whatever truth reaction you have discovered, go ahead and repeat it to yourself until you are able to accept that fact, regardless of whether you like the fact.

4. Tell the truth.

Once you are sure that you've found the radical truth, actually tell it to the person you are most afraid to tell. As you speak the truth face to face, see if you can remain connected to your inner lab. If you can't, that's okay. Just notice what happens. For example, before a meeting you might mention to Stephanie, "I realized the other day that I want to experience more power in my life."

5. Record your results.

Record how this process went for you: What was your truth reaction? How did you feel before, during, and after telling the truth? Did your energy increase? Did you gain any insights about your calling? For example, maybe Stephanie smiled in response to your statement and said, "What would you change, if you could?" The two of you got involved in an interesting conversation that ended up making you realize that you want to pursue creative writing outside of work. You notice that you no longer have the same "crush" response around Stephanie, though you still like and admire her. You actually become friends.

In addition to helping you find your truth reaction, the truth experiment helps you harness the *power* of authenticity. It turns the simple act of noticing an uncomfortable experience into a profound act of self-acceptance. It is rare that telling a deep truth to someone doesn't make you feel powerful.

You know, there's a reason you can even try the truth experiment at all. It's because you've successfully prepared your inner lab, you've worked with your fears, and you've begun to access the power of being in an authentic state. Nice work! For the final bit of work this week, let's ramp it up a bit.

The Wisdom of Your Superconscious

People have truth reactions even before they know what their bodies are trying to tell them. In one experiment, psychologists asked participants to draw a card from one of two card decks. The participants were supposed to get as many points as possible—but they didn't know that the researchers had stacked the decks so that one deck would consistently offer more points than the other. The psychologists wanted to know at what point people would realize that there was a good deck and a bad deck, and they also wanted to know what happened to people's bodies as they realized this.

It turned out that even before the participants drawing the cards consciously figured out that the decks were different, their bodies would respond differently when they were drawing cards from the good deck versus the bad deck (Bechara et al. 2005). This is true even in experiments in which there is no known subliminal way for people to figure out emotional or important future events (Mossbridge and Radin 2018a; Mossbridge and Radin 2018b). So it turns out that not only do our bodies help us confirm that something is important or interesting to us—they can do this even before we realize what is going on.

This sort of pre-event truth reaction can be thought of as a physiological equivalent to what some psychologists call your *superconscious wisdom.* The psychologist Roberto Assagioli and his students wrote about a portion of the mind that he called the "superconscious." He saw the superconscious as the source of intuitions that guide us toward positive outcomes; he also saw it as the source of our connection with the universe (Assagioli 1965). More on the universe in the last third of this course, but it's worth knowing that the idea of the superconscious is not just an idea— it's helpful to consider your superconscious to be at home in your body, right now. Even if you don't believe that the superconscious exists, it's easier to develop connections to something if you imagine it as real. In the final experiment of this week's work, you'll practice developing your connection to your superconscious and, at the same time, glean some clues about your calling.

⚗ The Listening Experiment

Goal: To develop a good relationship with your superconscious so that you can better receive clues about your calling.

Time requirement: 2 minutes each time you do it, ten to twenty times during the course of this week

To tap in to your superconscious, it's helpful to respond to questions very quickly. So this is a lightning-fill-in-the-blank experiment that you will repeat multiple times. You don't have to worry about being right, because you will do this exercise many times in the coming days. Try doing it three times a day, at breakfast, lunch, and dinner. Just have your lab notebook on hand during the week so you can record your answers.

This experiment consists of six fill-in-the-blank sentences you will complete as quickly as you can, over and over again. If you want to be really organized, you can write the sentences down in columns in your lab notebook, with one column for each blank you fill in, so that after doing the exercise ten to twenty times during the course of this week, you can see what is emerging in each column.

Each time you conduct this experiment, take the following steps:

1. Fill in the blanks.

    Begin by entering your inner lab and setting an intention to fill in the blanks in the sentences below, recording your answers in your lab notebook. Challenge yourself to fill in the blanks with the first thing that pops into your head—even if it doesn't make sense. Especially if it doesn't make sense!

    I love to _____.

    I feel best when _____.

    I remember being excited about _____.

    These days, I am learning how to _____.

    I hope it's not arrogant to believe that I can _____.

    It's probably not unique, but I think my calling might be related to _____.

2. Review your list.

    Once you're done with your ten to twenty fill-in-the-blank sessions, take a look at the list. Ask yourself which answers give you your truth reaction. Read those aloud to double-check. Notice especially your answers to the last two questions—these are set up specifically so that you can give yourself permission to get some initial insights about what your calling might be.

How did you feel doing this exercise? If you're like most people, you might be surprised at the answers at first, perhaps feeling as if they don't make sense. Later, you might have more insight about their meaning. That's great—it means you're allowing yourself to not consciously and immediately know all the answers. If, on the other hand, you don't have this experience, don't worry. It'll come. Ultimately, it's all about letting yourself really listen for clues to your calling without judgment.

You already worked last week on connecting to your intuition, and it's exciting to develop your connection to your superconscious—the source of your intuition, according to Assagioli. The more you practice connecting with your superconscious, the more you'll receive helpful intuitions. As you see this guidance working positively for you, you'll probably want to consult your superconscious again. It's a promising feedback loop, and you'll have a chance to work with your superconscious even more next week.

Conclusion

When you spend more time in an authentic state, the sludge hiding your true work from your awareness can begin to wash away. Though it may be hard to believe right now, your calling is already inside of you. It just needs a bit more time being fed by the power of your authenticity for you to really see and hear it with clarity—and working with your superconscious will help ramp up that clarity.

Speaking of power, next week you'll work on experiencing and experimenting with your authority as you improve your relationship with your superconscious. Your authority is the second most fundamental tool for discovering your true work, because when you are clear about where your authority begins and ends, you can focus your energy like a laser precisely on the work at hand.

Experimenting with Authority

Objective: To use your authority to create a first-pass definition of your calling by the end of this week.

The Domain of Your Absolute Authority

What is the domain of your absolute authority? In this program, the domain of your absolute authority encompasses what you have 100 percent control over. This domain excludes anything you do not have 100 percent control over. For example, you do not have 100 percent control over the weather, other people, the sounds you hear, the images you see, the movements you make, or the feelings you have. This massive lack of control isn't a failure on your part; it's true for everyone. The limits of your absolute authority are the same regardless of whether you are a billionaire, a baby, or an autocrat—part of the work this week is coming to this understanding.

Recognizing the domain of your absolute authority allows you to actually use your authority effectively. By the end of this week, you'll see that the effective use of your authority leads to everything that's ahead.

The Boundaries of Your Absolute Authority

To learn how to use your authority effectively, you'll need to concentrate it on what you have influence over. To get there, first we need to explore what is excluded from your absolute authority.

Everyone should agree that we don't have 100 percent control over our own bodies. If you disagree, let me know how you figured out how to have complete control over the biochemical and mechanical processes going on in that one lymph node on the left side of your neck! Everyone should also agree that we don't have 100 percent control over the contents of our thoughts and feelings. If you disagree, try testing yourself by reading these very words and not thinking about words. And if you say, "I could do that, but I don't want to," then let me know how you control what you want and don't want. Even long-term meditators don't claim to control all their thoughts and feelings—they observe them.

So if we don't have 100 percent control over our own bodies, thoughts, and feelings, it should be clear that we can't control the bodies, thoughts, and feelings of other people. What about inanimate objects? Well, we don't have 100 percent control over these either—if we did, we would make car keys appear when we needed them.

But let's go back to the "other people" part—because trying to control other people is something of a pastime for most of us, and it's important to get very clear that having 100 percent control over other people is not possible. In the discussion of authenticity last week, we looked at the habit of being inauthentic to try to control other people's behavior. You can also get in the habit of berating yourself when you aren't successful at controlling others—maybe you've thought to yourself, "I should have said something nice about her kids, but I didn't. That's probably why she didn't return my text message."

If you recognize these very common ways of being, it suggests that even if you are in an authentic state and you know that you can't actually control other people, some part of you still believes that your absolute authority extends to things that are outside of you. And this part of you defends itself by correctly pointing out that sometimes it feels like you really do influence others. In response, point out to this part of you that many factors influence how other people think and behave, and while a small percentage of these factors is your behavior, a much larger percentage consists of things like mood, personality, epigenetics, weather, stress level, and social status.

To really drive this point home, try this brief exercise to learn the boundaries of your absolute authority.

Brief Exercise

This exercise is a thought experiment to help you understand the boundaries of your absolute authority—don't actually do the things you imagine here.

1. Go into your inner lab and think of someone over whom you feel you have absolute authority.

2. In your mind, imagine doing whatever you need to do to get them to do exactly what you want. Maybe imagine threatening or bribing them.

3. Notice whether they follow your instructions. If so, does it feel like you have 100 percent control or authority over them? Or does it feel like they are scared or indebted to you, so they will do what you say only at this time?

4. Can you imagine a scenario in which someone would do exactly what you want them to do while also feeling as if they really want to do the thing you wanted them to do? If so, ask yourself if it seems as if they wanted to do those things in the first place. If yes, who has the actual authority: you or them?

5. Write in your lab notebook what you learned about the boundaries of your absolute authority.

Spending energy on attempting to control how others behave and think is a waste of valuable effort, and it rarely goes well. But spending energy on understanding the limits of your authority never goes unrewarded.

Non-Absolute Authority

If you accept the idea that you don't have 100 percent control over much, you probably still find yourself wondering what you do have 100 percent control over. Is there nothing inside the domain of your absolute authority? Yes, there's nothing inside the domain of your absolute authority. If the "you" we are talking about is your conscious self, you have 100 percent control over nothing. You may think you have 100 percent control over your choices, your attitude, your attention, or your desires. But even if you do have absolute authority over these things during your waking hours, all that goes away when you go to sleep.

Insight: You have 100 percent control over nothing.

Does all this mean you have no control at all? Nope. Does it mean you're at the mercy of everything else, that you don't get a vote at all? No, and no. It simply means that you don't have 100 percent control over anything.

But between 0 percent and 100 percent there's a lot of room for non-absolute authority. So what does this limited authority grant you? Limited authority gives you the power to use the authority you do have to decide whether you will follow the rules laid down by any higher authority. Granted, the consequences for not following these rules may not be good. But your authority, if only to have your own thoughts and feelings and nothing else, still exists squarely within you. And if you concentrate that authority within your authentic self, you will have the most authority possible.

Concentrating Your Authority in Your Authentic Self

In the next brief exercise, we'll work on concentrating your limited authority where it counts—in your authentic self. What does it mean to concentrate your authority within your authentic self? It means to include all parts of you in your authentic self—your conscious mind, your superconscious, all parts of your unconscious mind, and your body. All of them, working together as your authentic self, will direct your actions.

You don't have to be conscious of exactly how you direct your actions. But you do need to enlarge your definition of your authentic self until it covers all parts of you and it excludes anything that's not you.

Why enlarge your definition of your authentic self? Because if you do, your entire authentic self will have absolute authority—100 percent control—over what goes on in your inner space. What seems here like a trick is not really a trick at all. It's just that the definition of "you" changed. At first, "you" was your conscious mind. Conscious-mind-you didn't have control over your thoughts and feelings because conscious-mind-you was not able to control the factors that affected them. But when "you" includes your conscious mind, your superconscious, your unconscious, and your body—all bundled together in your authentic self—this new and greater you has 100 percent authority over itself. While conscious-mind-you still won't be in control of your larger authentic self, when you combine your body with your conscious mind, your superconscious, and your unconscious, at least one component of this greater, bundled authentic self will be in charge. And that means your inner space is completely yours.

Insight: When your authentic self contains all your authority, no one can touch your authority over your inner space.

Brief Exercise

Take a moment now to grow and redefine the boundaries of your authentic self.

1. Record in your lab notebook how you feel now, before you begin.

2. Take a moment to relax and breathe, then go into your inner lab.

3. Once you feel centered there, simply ask your superconscious to reveal any parts of you—as represented by any feelings you might have—that are left alone, not included in your authentic self. You don't have to name these parts of you, just let them appear. They can be your conscious mind, your superconscious itself, your unconscious mind, your body, or other parts.

4. Make sure each part belongs to you and is not borrowed from someone else. A good bet is to first ask if the part wants to come home to you.

5. Talk to each of these parts of you. Tell each one you'd like them to come back home.

6. Explore how you might join up with each part of you. Each part might need something unique, so have a conversation with each one. Here are some questions to ask of each part:

   • What do you feel?

   • What would make you feel okay about joining the rest of me?

7. Ask yourself, "Can I commit to trying to give this part what it needs?" If the answer to this last question is yes, imagine giving the part what it needs—an hour of time each day, really good food, whatever the case may be—and see how the part responds. If the answer is no, keep talking to the part and negotiate a compromise that works for both of you. When you have a

compromise, imagine giving the part what you've agreed upon and see how this part of yourself responds.

8. When you are done talking with all the parts that have shown up, record how you feel in your lab notebook.

Beginning to collect all of what belongs to you into your authentic self is a powerful practice, and you'll put that power to good use. Later this week, you'll use the authority of your larger, redefined authentic self to get some additional clarity about your calling. But first, it's important to explore what childhood lessons you might have learned about using your authority.

Jonathan: Childhood Lessons on Authority

"Jonathan Moreno, the son of the pioneers who perfected the use of psychodrama in group therapy" is exactly how Dr. Moreno knew he didn't want his obituary to read. Jonathan received several gifts from the unusual experience of growing up as the son of a famous psychiatrist and a psychologist, including a childhood that involved world travel, the media spotlight, and unusually close contact with mentally ill people. This array of experiences brought a mix of feelings and insights. Jonathan learned about the wishes of his authentic self: (1) he wanted to have his own success, separate from his parents' fame, (2) he wanted a "normal" life for his kids, and (3) he wished he could teach others that different people and different cultures have markedly distinct perspectives, all to try to understand and deal with the difficult experience of being human.

Jonathan says that although he didn't go to a "fancy" college or graduate school, he has been single-minded about his purpose, which is to transmit ideas that promote human flourishing. Objectively it seems he has been successful at this, as he is now a bioethicist, philosopher, and professor.

For Jonathan, it was more than helpful to have unusual childhood experiences, even with their drawbacks, because these experiences helped him see that he was a unique person just like the people who worked with his parents in therapy groups. The early emphasis on different perspectives challenged him at an early age to define what his own perspective was. He learned about authenticity by recognizing the differences between himself and his parents, and he saw that he could only use his authority when he had access to his authentic self. Without those insights, it is likely that Jonathan would have found the process of becoming who he is today much more difficult. Of course, not everyone grew up in such a yeasty environment, but each of us has something we have learned about our authority from our childhood experiences.

Along these lines, my father suffered from obsessive-compulsive disorder to the extent that he would floss my teeth and those of my sister's every night for forty-five minutes to an hour, per child. This is not a childhood misrepresentation of time; I know this because he also recorded these flossing sessions on ninety-minute audio tapes, and they didn't always fit into that time constraint. He would ignore our complaints and attempts to reason with him. This seemed like bizarre nightly torture, but he did it because he was convinced our mouths were dirty.

This difficult nightly ritual taught me a very clear lesson about my authority. I learned that while I didn't have any authority over my father or much authority over my own mouth, I did have limited (not 100 percent) authority over my thoughts, feelings, and behavior. At times, I could let myself feel angry at my father. And, for the most part, I could avoid thanking him for flossing my teeth or acting like it was normal for him to floss my teeth so obsessively. That was how I used my authority, when I could—I tried to stay connected to my authentic self even as he distanced himself from his own, so that I could retain the little bit of authority I did have. I think it's one of the things that saved me.

Now I extend my authority to include in my authentic self my whole body and all parts of my mind—and the power I feel is tremendous. You can reeducate yourself as well by taking a curious look at your childhood experiences.

Brief Exercise

This activity is about examining what your childhood experiences taught you about using your authority.

1. Get out your lab notebook.

2. List three to four important childhood experiences. These are your funny or tragic well-worn stories, the ones you bring up in conversations with friends or in therapy.

3. Go through each item on the list and ask yourself, "From this experience, what did my child-self learn about using my authority?"

4. Write briefly about your overall childhood lessons regarding using your authority. Did you learn that you couldn't use your authority outside your home? That you had to use your authority in inappropriate ways? That you could use partial authority over your body but not your mind? Vice versa?

5. Complete this sentence: Right now, using my authority feels _____.

6. Finally, complete this sentence: I would like to feel that using my authority is _____. Just writing down how you would like to feel about using your authority is enough to begin your reeducation.

All this work on authority is directed toward one thing: getting more clues about the shape of your true work. By now, you're ready to make a rough sketch of your calling. Let's get to it.

Using Your Authority to Listen for Your Calling

Remember the Listening Experiment from last week? If you did not do that experiment, stop now, do it, then come back here.

Turn to the pages in your lab notebook where you wrote your answers to the fill-in-the-blank questions. Where did these answers come from? Let's assume they came from the superconscious—the part of you that delivers useful intuitions. You might wonder, "If there's a part of me that has that wisdom, why didn't it just come out and tell me about my calling?" One way to reconcile this is that your superconscious has been waiting a long time to become part of you. And now you've welcomed your superconscious into your authentic self. You are ready to use the authority of your larger authentic self to begin defining your calling in earnest.

The way you'll do this in the clarifying-your-calling experiments is to say different versions of your calling out loud, so you can sense your truth reaction. Why "out loud"? Because using our voices and listening to them allows us to figure out if we are telling the truth. Researchers who study lie detection say that both the words that are used when a person speaks out loud as well as the tone of voice are very useful tools for determining the truth (DePaulo and Morris 2004). Most people know the truth when they hear it. You are going to use that skill now, in this next experiment. You'll say some words about your calling and ask your superconscious to keep delivering messages until one sounds true.

⚗ The Clarifying-Your-Calling Experiment, Version 1

Goal: To clarify your calling.

Time required: 15–20 minutes

This experiment is not the ultimate clarification of your calling. You have a whole program to finish, and by the time it's done, your calling will be much clearer. For now, this experiment is about getting a brief, relatively clear description of your calling. To prepare for this experiment, get your lab notebook and turn to the pages where you wrote your responses to the Listening Experiment.

1. Go into your inner lab.

Feel your authentic self, and remind yourself that it now contains all parts of your body and mind. From these parts, send a special invite to your superconscious to come sit in your laboratory for a while.

2. Ask for help.

Ask your superconscious to help you gain clarity about your calling during the rest of this experiment. How does your superconscious respond? Does it agree? If not, have a conversation with it to get to a comfortable agreement.

3. Consolidate your data.

Look through your answers to the Listening Experiment. Consider them all. What are the thoughts about your calling that bubble up when you read through these answers? Write them in your lab notebook. If you are having trouble, do the speedy fill-in-the-blanks activity again with these sentences:

It seems like my calling has something to do with _____.

My calling can't be _____ because that's too simple.

I sure seem to love to _____, but how can that be a calling?

4. Write down your results.

Talk a bit more with your superconscious, then ask it to get connected to the part of your mind that writes. Don't worry about how it will do that, just ask it to do that. Then go ahead and let it write out the completion of this sentence.

My calling is _____.

5. Listen for truth.

Gather your authentic self together by imagining you are in a sphere containing all of your mind and body. Say the sentence you have written in step 4 in your full voice. Listen for truth as you say it. If you feel your truth reaction and the power of your calling, you are done for now. Nice work! If you don't feel your truth reaction and the power of your calling, go back into your inner laboratory. Ask your superconscious to try again, and let it know you will be patient—you'll keep asking until you correctly receive the message that is true. Then go back to step 3 and fill in the blanks there again. Keep doing steps 3 through 5 until you feel your truth reaction and the power of your calling—you will know when you feel both of them.

When you are in your full authority of your authentic self and in real collaboration with your superconscious, the message will be clear, true, and powerful. But give this collaboration some time if it feels like it's not working out. And consider doing the alternative experiment below if you get really stuck.

⚗ The Clarifying-Your-Calling Experiment, Version 2

Goal: To clarify your calling.

Time required: 15–20 minutes

Try this experiment if the first one didn't work for you or if you just want another chance to further define your calling. Remember, you are free to do whatever works for you. Have fun!

1. Go into your inner lab.

Feel your authentic self, and remind yourself that it now contains all parts of your body and mind. From these parts, send a special invite to your superconscious to come sit in your laboratory for a while.

2. What makes you feel alive?

    In your lab notebook, write down one thing you've done—job, hobby, sport, activity, anything—that makes you feel in love with life. If there is more than one thing, write that down. Write down everything you can think of that has made you feel alive. Remember not to force these toward the Mother Theresa end of the spectrum. Watching reality TV should go on this list if these shows leave you feeling energized and in love with life.

3. Change elements of each.

    Now read through the list of one or more things that make you feel alive. Take each one and imagine that it is changed slightly. Remove elements of it, piece by piece, until it becomes something you don't think you'd love anymore. Notice what you have to take away for it to become something you wouldn't love. For example, a carpenter I know loves to do carpentry, but if it weren't for the feeling of the wood under his hands, he'd no longer love it.

4. Find the essential part of each.

    Write down next to each item on your list what you couldn't remove from it without losing your love for it. These are parts of your calling; they are your passions. For example, the carpenter I know would list: the smell of sawdust, manual labor, the feel of wood. Look through the list of passions and ask yourself what they have in common. Try out several ideas to see how they feel to you. If you find a description of a more global passion, write it down. For the carpenter, a more global passion would be woodworking with his own hands. It's also fine to have more than one passion.

5. Meditate on your calling and declare it.

    Gather your authentic self together by imagining you are in a sphere containing all of your mind and body. Spend a few minutes right now meditating on what you think your calling might be, given your passion or passions. Notice how you feel as you are doing this. Do you feel a bit off center? Then go back to what you wrote down in steps 3 and 4, and recheck your work by making sure it all feels true. On the other hand, if you feel at home in the full authority of your authentic self, then you are ready to complete the following sentence, allowing whatever arises.

My calling is _____.

Read this sentence out loud, and watch for your truth reaction.

You should come out of either experiment with a statement of your calling as you understand it now. If not, redo one or the other on another day this week, remembering to gather the full authority of your authentic self as you do them.

Congratulations! Having a better sense of your calling usually feels like a relief. That's partly because the process of discovering your true work requires having the experience of making yourself much larger than you're used to being. There's power in including all of you in your authentic self, and you've now felt that power.

Conclusion

Stop for a moment and appreciate the beauty of this first statement of your calling. For inspiration, here are some examples of callings, from some of the beautiful people I have known, talked to, and worked with:

To sing in a clear, authentic voice

To help people laugh and forgive

To amplify women's voices

To teach people how to love their gardens

To remind people about the importance of their families

To draw cartoons that remind people of their humanity

To make the environment safe for humans and animals

To create robots that teach people how to be better humans

To help animals find homes

These examples don't include feeding the poor, healing the sick, or mediating governmental conflict. Yet they are all important in the working of the world.

If you can't immediately see how your current sense of your calling will manifest in the world, that's to be expected. Defining your calling is getting clear about what makes you come alive; you have the rest of this program to figure out how you'll bring that aliveness to the world. Next week, you'll discover some of the unique details of your calling, and you'll even make some headway toward pursuing it, all thanks to the helpful tool of *choice*.

WEEK 4

Your Choice, Your Calling

Objective: To define your calling and take it out for a brief spin, once you've examined how choice works for you.

Your Relationship with Choice

You've almost made it to the end of the first part of the Calling program! It's a huge chunk of work. If you were a graduate student in a PhD program, you'd be finishing up your dissertation and looking forward to your postdoctoral project (part II).

What remains is to do an experimental test of your calling so that you can move on to understanding and pursuing it fully. To really step into the emotional work it takes to commit to a final definition of your calling, you need to examine your relationship with choice. Going forward, how you make choices will have a tremendous influence on your ability to get your soul's work under way in the world. This week we will take the time to look with curiosity at your relationship with choice, so you can choose with your whole self how to put your calling to the test.

The Marshmallow Test

You might have heard of the "marshmallow test" (e.g., Mischel 2014), the psychology experiment in which a kid is left alone in a room with a marshmallow and is told that if they are able to not eat the marshmallow until the time the experimenter returns, they will get two marshmallows. It's supposed to be a test of self-control and the ability to delay gratification. To get the "better" prize (two marshmallows), the child must control their urge to eat the one marshmallow on the plate in front of them, delaying their pleasure to get a bigger reward. At some point, most kids learn to wait for the second marshmallow, but in the early years, this is very difficult for them.

This is really an experiment about choice. Let's look at it carefully, through a microscope. Imagine a four-year-old who likely has a difficult time with this task. He sits on his hands, squirming, as he tries not to eat the marshmallow. Within a few minutes, he gives up and eats it. We look at this scenario and we say, "He tried to have self-control, but eventually he chose to have one marshmallow now rather than have to wait for two." We make an assumption that he made a choice, because he is old enough to understand and try to follow directions but not old enough to be able to wait.

Okay, now let's imagine a six-month-old in the same situation. You might say this is completely unfair—a baby can't follow directions or control herself—but let's imagine it anyway. The six-month-old drools all over the marshmallow, and maybe she drops it on the floor. Of course, the six-month-old didn't choose anything. She just did what came naturally. We might say she couldn't have made a choice, because she doesn't have the resources required to make a choice, which include understanding the situation, acting skillfully, and being able to predict the outcomes of her actions.

Finally, let's imagine a normally functioning thirty-five-year-old in the same experiment (with marshmallows replaced by money). She hears the explanation, the experimenter leaves the room, and she meditates, naps, or stares into space until the experimenter comes back in and offers extra money as a reward for her patience. We observe this and assume that she was capable of making a choice, she could wait, and in the end she made the best choice.

These stories about choice are similar to the stories we have about how we live our lives ("Why couldn't I just wait?" "I should have said something else." "I'm so glad I chose to go to that party!"). But given what we know about how the brain works, it seems that two of the three marshmallow-test stories are wrong. The only story that really reflects what is going on for us in the rest of our lives is the one about the six-month-old. We are in many ways like the baby, in every choice we make. That's because our brain is always trying its best, given the information and the abilities it has.

Every Choice Is the Best Choice, Given the Circumstances

Bear with me as I stake out an explanation for this seemingly radical statement. First, like a six-month-old, we often don't comprehend at least one of the crucial factors governing the situations in which we find ourselves. Second, even as adults, we don't always have the capacity to take the most effective actions we would like, and we are often wrong about predicting the outcomes of the actions we do manage to take. Third, and most important, our desired outcomes might not even be the best ones for us!

For instance, we generally say the four-year-old made a bad choice. But it is also possible that if he had waited and gotten to eat the second marshmallow, he might have felt sick. And what would we say the best choice was, if that happened? We might say that the thirty-five-year-old made the best choice because she received a monetary bonus. Yet, had she not received the extra money and gone shopping at the mall, she might have instead spent the day relaxing at the beach, where she might have met a wonderful new friend. The point is, even when we think we know all the factors, and we think we know what the best outcome would be, we still don't really know what our best choice is. *We always have to guess.*

This idea can be hard to swallow. The first time I introduce it to people, they tend to balk. After all, our whole legal system and many of our social norms are based on the idea that conscious, intelligent adults choose our behaviors. But that doesn't mean we know what our best choices are at any one time.

Have you ever wished intently, day after day, for a particular acceptance letter from a college or employer, only to get rejected? You wanted to be admitted to the school or hired by the company, and you were sure it was the best choice for you, for many reasons. You checked your messages constantly, hoping to see some indication of your acceptance. Finally, when you got the rejection letter, you were in grief. You were just miserable. Nothing could be good again.

Looking back on it now, though, you might feel grateful. If you had gone to that college or taken that job, you wouldn't have the friends or work that you have now. So, in retrospect, you wonder if that really would have been the best choice for you, or if it just looked that way from the ground, when you didn't have the bird's eye view you have now. The facts you had at the time are locked into history. What's different now is that you have more information about your life. Does it make sense now that every choice we make is the best choice, given what we know and are capable of at the time?

> **Insight:** Every choice we make is the best choice we can make, given what we know and are capable of at the time we choose.

We are always operating with the best information that we could possibly have, given the circumstances, and our choices are exactly as informed as they can be in the moment. I am not kidding about this. Even making the choice to do self-harm or hurt others, or any other serious action that changes the course of our lives, is still made given the best of our abilities at the moment we make them. These abilities may be crappy, but they are the best we have at a given time.

All this is to say that the point of really putting your choices under a microscope isn't to beat yourself up about past choices, because you really were trying as hard as you could given the information you had at the time. Rather, the point I'm making is about focusing on the future and the choices you will make going forward. It's worth recognizing that you can improve your ability to assess life situations, guess at the best outcome, and take effective actions that are likely to lead toward that outcome. And you don't need to get better at all three of these areas at once. There's really just one thing you need to practice: making choices with all of yourself.

Splintered Paths

One of the most difficult things for passionate graduate students to learn is that they can't do every study or perform every bit of research that interests them. They have to choose, and then they have to throw their whole selves into the choice.

"Oh my God, just commit to one study and do it!" one of my advisers said after I had presented five or more different exciting options for a new experiment. Although we must all learn to *do* many things in our lives, she was talking about *making a choice*. When you're making a choice, you necessarily choose one path—until the next option comes along, when you make another choice.

> **Insight:** At any moment, to choose is necessarily to reject all forward paths but one.

There's great wisdom in her emphatic advice. When you fail to really choose, life moves forward and you end up feeling like you are in many places at once—as if you are spread across *splintered paths*.

The idea that we have many paths—of family, career, spirituality, money, politics, friendship, and more—is a popular one. The prevailing belief is that we must balance all these paths, so that we move along all of them simultaneously and equally. It's a compelling idea, because we can sense the need to balance all the complicated parts of our lives and ourselves. Many of us strive to be an integrated person—someone who meshes together all these parts and considers each of these paths with each step.

But actually, in a truly integrated person, these paths aren't separated in any way at all. Each of these different areas of your life supports you in bringing your true work to the world. Good relationships, a satisfying career, enough money, good health, and psychological well-being support your happiness and the pursuit of your calling. Ask yourself which is easier: attending to all of those paths or attending to a single one? When I discovered my calling— to teach and learn about love and time—and I decided to commit to that calling, I began to see a single path emerge. It was much, much, much easier to balance things—because I didn't have to balance anything at all. It's as if making a choice that commits you to the path of your true work integrates all these different aspects of yourself, without you having to try. One step on your true path beats a million steps on the other paths all apart.

Insight: Only one path will do; it's the path of your true work.

Why do we stay on splintered paths if they make our lives less effective? Well, moving on one path at a time is often a good way to move closer to a short-term, societally validated goal. You can make the career change you think you want (career path), so you will be recognized by your peers the way you want to be (status path). Then, that puts you in a higher income bracket (money path), which means you're in a better position to find the kind of romantic relationship you want (love path). It seems integrated because movement on your different paths is linked. Moving on each of our splintered paths can feel right for a brief time. But when you commit to one path—your true path—things in your life become less like an arduous puzzle and more like a delightful hike.

For the sake of argument, let's say you move farther down each of your splintered paths. What happens is that you can start to forget there is any other way to move at all. None of this would be a problem, except that by moving forward across multiple splintered paths you dilute your resources and yourself. As a result, not only do you have less energy for any of your paths, it's much more difficult to access the power of your authentic self or your full authority. And as that power disappears, so does your ability to pursue your calling.

You may not be traveling on splintered paths right now, but it's worth asking yourself several questions about the path you happen to be on. Do you feel cut off from yourself? Did you notice that you discovered your calling last week and are not feeling committed to it? Are you unaware of where you are and what you are feeling right now? Do you do too much and wonder if all your effort is worth it? Have you lately been sick, depressed, or lonely?

If you answer yes to any of these questions, it does not necessarily mean you are spread across splintered paths. These symptoms can of course result from other causes. But being spread too thin across splintered paths is a very common problem, and it can result in all of these symptoms. I know this from experience.

A Splintered Mommy Path

After my son was born and my husband went back to work, I was in charge of taking care of our new baby all day. I quickly became depressed, and I didn't know why. I thought that it certainly couldn't be because of the baby. After all, I loved my son and felt nothing but pleasure in being his mom. Or so I thought. That belief was coming from a splintered "mommy path." On this path, I was supposed to feel nothing but pleasure in being a mother and in loving my son—and no other feelings were allowed. Yet there was another, equally real path on which I was not a mother at all and was pursuing graduate school and a dissertation about perceptual learning in the auditory system—and no other feelings were allowed.

When I began to realize that the cause of my depression was that I had split myself across at least two different paths, I went into my inner lab and had a discussion with the parts of myself that were on each of those paths. I realized I felt anger about being completely responsible for another person, my son. I also felt grief about losing my old life, in which I'd had more time to think about intriguing ideas. I also discovered new, joyful feelings in the life I was living now. I felt excited to learn what my son was like, how our relationship would turn out, and what being a mother was all about. I spent time listening to and allowing myself to admit to all of my feelings.

Once I had admitted to myself that all my feelings were legitimate, a solution came to me. I called up my dissertation adviser and told her I would be returning part-time to finish up my dissertation, staying at home with my son the rest of the time. That action, borne from listening to all of myself and taking all of my feelings seriously, put me on my way back to a single, joyful path.

Suzanne: Uniting Splintered Paths

Suzanne Clores is a podcast producer, fiction and nonfiction author, and essayist. Her calling is to create an open discussion about psychic functioning and self-expression. When I asked her to voice her calling, she said, "To get the conversation about psychic experiences and how they fit into my psychological landscape out into the world. What are my episodes and experiences and why can't I let them go? I'm looking for some type of resolution, and I think it will help people. Now that I say that out loud, it's very scary that I've chosen that, because I'm resistant to shining light on it. Just now, it suddenly seems like a bad idea!"

We talked about her resistance to voicing her calling, and she told me that as a child her family pushed her to perform. She hated the experience of being pushed to be in front of others, and to avoid that experience she went the other direction—she became a writer at least partly to escape being seen. Writing helped her be more comfortable, but it also shut down her voice, in a way, by narrowing her possibilities as well as her skill set. It's as if she put part of herself on a narrow writer's path, which didn't include using her voice. Meanwhile, she loved to sing and talk with others, and she started toying with the idea of creating a podcast about extraordinary experiences. One foot in front of the other, and she's already working on planning another season of her podcast, The Extraordinary Project.

Through working with a voice teacher as well as making other changes in her life, Suzanne called part of herself back from her narrowly visioned writer's path. She can still write as part of her work, and she will always do so—but her true work is not strictly about writing. It's about doing everything that it takes to get a particular conversation, a difficult and controversial conversation, out into the world. And she's even open to changes in her calling if they show up on her unitary path.

When I asked her what she would say to her younger self, a ten-year-old girl who felt a passion for writing, she said, "Rather than trying to hide, don't rule out the idea that you can still be big. And that could be fun. Play more. Don't be afraid to exhibit the playful part of your voice and being. Find supportive environments. Say what you are excited about. You're glorious! Full of energy and power and potential. You're already doing it and being it. This is it! Rest in grace. I love you."

What does it feel like to travel on a single path? It feels like your energy is no longer dissipating. It feels like your authority remains in your authentic self while your path forward is unitary and joyful. Sound good? Great! Let's make it so.

Brief Exercise

This is a practice for any time you sense you have some splintered paths. It bundles your trajectories together into a single, unitary path.

1. Go into your inner lab and get out your lab notebook.

2. Draw a central circle in your lab notebook and label it "authentic self." Remind yourself that this includes your entire mind and body.

3. From your authentic self, draw a line going out like a spoke on a wheel. Ask your superconscious what to label this line—this is one of your splintered paths. It could be "work" or "dance career" or "parenting" or "taking care of the elderly." It's just the name of one of the paths in your life that does not include all of your paths.

4. Keep repeating step 3 until you have all your splintered paths represented.

5. On a new page in your lab notebook, draw a circle at the bottom of the page and label it "authentic self." Again, remind yourself that this includes your entire mind and body.

6. From your authentic self, draw one line—you might want to make it wide—to represent a single path.

7. On that line, place any of the splintered paths that you want to include in your single, joyful path.

8. Once you have included all of your paths, label the new path forward "my unitary path."

9. Request that your superconscious help keep your path unitary so that it includes all of your steps.

10. Write down how you feel about this process in your lab notebook.

Moving forward on a single path allows your future choices to be simpler, because you don't have to worry about their effects on a whole array of splintered paths. You're ready to harness that simplicity as you finish out this week experimenting with your true work.

The Next Choice: Experimenting with Your Calling

Last week, you bundled all of your mind and body into your authentic self, and you increased your authority as a result. This week, you bundled your splintered paths into a unitary path. Having the full authority of your authentic self and a single, unitary path forward are the two ingredients needed to make choices with all of yourself. And now, you'll do exactly that. Starting with the very next choice you make.

You don't have to master everything you've learned to continue. It's enough to have considered these ideas and tried the exercise. You will continue to integrate yourself and your path during the course of this program and beyond. For now, it's time to use what you have learned to choose something exciting: your way of experimenting with your calling. This is the first of two "calling experiments" in the program, so we'll name it Calling Experiment 1.

⚗ Calling Experiment 1

Goal: To choose your own way of experimenting with your true work.

Time required: 1 to 2 hours

This experiment does more to bring you closer to testing out your calling than any experiment or exercise you've done so far. That's because it helps you take your newfound wisdom right out into the world, in the same way a newly minted PhD might. You need to experiment with what you've discovered on your own terms and in ways that you invent.

This experiment can seem complicated, so consider reading it all the way through before starting it.

1. Brainstorm.

    Get out your lab notebook, hang out in your inner laboratory, and brainstorm questions about the logistics of your calling. For example, you might wonder how your calling is supposed to actually work, whether you have to quit your job, how you're going to find the money, who will help you, whether there is a particular subset of your true work that you could start with, and so on. Just list all of the questions about your calling that you have. When you feel you're about done, look through the list and circle one question that is currently begging you to answer it. As you do this, it's good to remember that all of these questions need answers. You're just choosing one right now, and you're trying to choose with your whole self. That circled question is the question that you will now begin to address in the next step.

2. Use your intuition to plan your experiment.

    Now you have your question—but how to address it? This is when you need to draw on, once again, your blooming collaboration with your superconscious mind. Ask your superconscious mind to join you again in your inner lab to help you plan this experiment. Imagine that your superconscious is giving you a gift. Without thinking, look at what it is offering you. If you don't see anything, just notice what thoughts you are thinking. Write down or draw that gift or the first object, person, activity, or idea that you think of (if you saw no gift) in your lab notebook. This will be your gift. Now, next to your gift, write down your circled question. Under the question, do some free association to develop your potential directions for this step. What does your gift remind you of? How could this association address your question?

All this may sound complicated, so here's an example: Steve, whose calling is to educate young children to better understand themselves and others, sees his superconscious in his inner lab, but he doesn't really see a gift. He notices that there's this irrepressible thought about a comb that keeps coming into his head. He ignores his own skepticism and judgment, writing down "comb" and sketching a rough image of a comb in his lab notebook. Next, he writes down his circled question next to the comb, which was "How will I transition from working with adults as a corporate lawyer to working with children as an educator?" Then he writes his associations with "comb." They turn into these ways to address his question:

Combing my contacts to find educators to interview.

Combs for head lice! Changing my caseload to focus on companies serving children.

Combining my abilities in law with my desire to educate.

In this way, you can see how something as unconventional and random as "comb" can lead someone to a completely unexpected insight.

3. Plan your experiment.

Go to your list of ways to address the question. Take a moment to make sure you are traveling on a single, unitary path. With the full authority of your authentic self, circle the way to address the question that seems most promising. Remember that all these ways of addressing the question could be useful and may be part of your answer—but for now just choose one, from the full authority of your authentic self, with the intention of keeping your path a unitary one.

Now take a look at what you circled and plan a simple experiment from it, with a goal related to understanding how this direction feels. Keep your experiment very simple, something you could comfortably complete in an hour or so. Then in your lab notebook, write down a title for your experiment, a goal, a plan, and how you will interpret the results.

Let's go back to Steve's process as an example: Steve circles "Combs for head lice!" and decides to perform a simple experiment testing out this direction. In his lab notebook, he writes down his goal, his plan, and how he'll interpret his results.

> **Experiment:** Kids' Companies!
>
> **Goal:** To see how it feels to move closer to my calling and to continue deepening my relationship with my superconscious mind.
>
> **Plan:** To spend an hour going through my portfolio and checking online to determine whether any of my clients have children's divisions.
>
> **Interpretation:** If I feel more alive when I do this experiment than I do in my daily work, I'll interpret this as indicating that this direction might be fruitful for me. If I feel less alive or if I feel frustrated, this will tell me that this approach may not be fruitful or that it must be changed in some way.

4. Perform your experiment and record the results.

    You know how to do this—you just wrote down your plan! Now go do your experiment, observe yourself as you do it, and record the results. Take note of whether you lost sight of your authority or whether you drifted away from authenticity during your experiment; these might be important clues to what needs to be changed or improved in your statement of your calling, depending on your interpretation of the results.

5. Celebrate yourself.

    Woo-hoo! You did it! Here you are, walking on a single path, pursuing your calling! You tried out an idea about your true work and you learned something. Do something nice to celebrate your amazing progress. There will be so much more!

You can see your soul's work as a series of experiments that will never end. The experiment you just created and performed is just the beginning, and you'll pick up the thread of this work in the third portion of this program, after you get your calling supercharged.

Conclusion

Congratulations, graduate! Now...it's time for more work! You've worked remarkably well with your intuition, authenticity, authority, and the power of choice to get to this moment. There might be a desire to zoom ahead and unleash your calling on the world. You could stop the program now and do that. This would be like graduating with your PhD and deciding to not get any more training.

Avoid the temptation! Generations of scientists will tell you it's well worth going deeper—to hone your awareness and abilities so when it's time for you to launch your calling in the world, you have the understanding and the skills you need.

PART II

Energize Your Calling

Welcome to your postdoctoral weeks! Now that you've said it out loud and written it down, you have a much clearer sense of your soul's work; if someone were to ask you what your calling is, you'd be able to tell them. And you've also taken some steps toward experimenting with your calling.

Whether your true work is to find animals new homes, create beautiful music, give comfort to the sick, create spaces for businesses, or help people remember their parents' lives, you can't get it all done right away, and you can't get it done alone. It takes a team to energize your calling. But it also takes more than a team—it takes deep self-awareness, trust, love, and a plan for managing your own shortcomings and gifts.

Here in part II, you'll do exercises and experiments that will help you energize your calling. During the next four weeks, you will call together a group of supportive people, learn to trust yourself and others, love your shortcomings, and become very clear about the gifts your calling brings to the world. At the end of this part of the program, you'll have what amounts to a practical *user's guide* to your calling that you can reference; consider it a troubleshooting guide for any future difficulties on your path.

Preparing Your Calling Circle

Objective: To invite at least one person into your calling circle after investigating who resonates with you and working with your anger.

Your Calling Circle

You can't do your true work on your own. Period. No one can. This is powerful stuff; you're working with your calling here. You need support, and now is the time to get it in the form of your team, your *calling circle*.

A calling circle is a group of two or more people who support each other in staying in the full authority of their authentic selves, moving forward on unitary paths, and generally understanding and pursuing their true work. This week's work is about beginning to create the calling circle that will support you for the rest of this program.

Before you run screaming in fear that you'll have to build a community in a week, it's worth knowing that all you need to start your calling circle is one other person who resonates with you. That's the only commitment that you'll make this week: finding at least one person who resonates with you and your calling.

Finding One Who Resonates

Being connected to one person who can really accept and appreciate who we are has a profound impact on our lives. In fact, according to a study by the United States' National Scientific Council on the Developing Child, "Despite the widespread belief that individual grit, extraordinary self-reliance, or some in-born, heroic strength of character can triumph over calamity, science now tells us that it is the reliable presence of at least one supportive relationship and multiple opportunities for developing effective coping skills that are essential building blocks for the capacity to do well in the face of significant adversity" (2015, 7).

That's right—we need that one supportive relationship, and we need challenges to prepare ourselves for difficulty. Luckily, life gives everyone challenges. Supportive relationships, however, can be difficult to find, even though they are absolutely essential.

Jesse: Loved into Aliveness

Jesse* is a popular psychoanalyst and professor at the Institute for Psychoanalysis, in Chicago. Her calling is to listen deeply to people and, by listening, to heal them. Even though she was in her late seventies when I interviewed her, she was still seeing clients for about thirty hours a week. Throughout her years, she's been in recovery from extreme neglect by her parents as well as from her own alcoholism, among other troubles. When I asked about her purpose, she spoke especially to the power of people bringing each other into aliveness, through being with each other authentically.

At first, Jesse brought up the children's story The Velveteen Rabbit, *in which a child loves a toy rabbit so much that the rabbit becomes alive. Jesse said she feels that she was "loved into aliveness" much the same way. She explained that when she was seven or eight years old, she was on the floor near a rocking chair where her aunt was sitting and drinking coffee.* "*She wasn't speaking at all, but the way she looked at me—I knew that my aunt, in that moment, could take me in. I felt seen for the first time. She was free from her own psychological stuff going on, and she could really see me.*"

As Jesse spoke about the experience, she cried a little, saying, "*She sat there in that God-damned rocking chair, and without a word communicated to me that I was seen and she knew who I was. At that moment, I knew there was that kind of love and connection to be had in the universe.*" Jesse came to the conclusion, later in our interview, that this is the exact experience that she has been repeating with her clients ever since that moment on the floor being seen and heard by her aunt. She loves her clients into aliveness, often without a word. Often just by listening for their authentic selves.

Of course, like all of us, Jesse sometimes slips out of connection with others. Losing this connection is, for Jesse, losing her capacity to fulfill her calling. I asked Jesse what she does to continue to work toward her calling when she's feeling separated from her ability to connect with others. She said, "*Well, when I was drinking, I couldn't connect to people, because I couldn't connect to myself. I had to stop drinking to reconnect with myself and others. And other times, when I'm with a client, if I can't feel the connection with them I just tell them. I say, 'I can't feel you' and then we figure it out.*

"*I used to feel like I didn't exist if I couldn't connect to others, but I've been loved enough by people important to me that now I feel like I still exist even when I can't connect to someone else. The state of being connected to my purpose is, for me, the state of being able to listen deeply and connect; that state by definition includes both people. The channel is cocreated—it's only the 'twoness' of it that creates seeing and being seen.*"

Jesse's experience of this "twoness" is something that many of us crave, especially if we didn't experience it as children. We often search for it in romantic relationships, and some of us find it there.

But this kind of experience doesn't have to be reserved for romance. True support can occur in relationships of all kinds: friendships, work relationships, and family relationships.

Insight: We all need at least one relationship with someone who supports us in being our authentic selves.

Feeling like we are seeing and being seen, listening and being heard, is the essence of a calling circle, and it is easier to create than you might think. Who in your life could serve this vital function? Let's find out. We'll start with this brief exercise to help you brainstorm who is (and isn't) a good candidate for your calling circle.

Brief Exercise

Let's make a quick list of people you already know who you will and will not consider for your calling circle.

1. Get your lab notebook out and welcome yourself into your inner lab.

2. Once you feel centered there, write a list of all the people you know, including those close to you and those who are just acquaintances. For now, just let the names come without judgment, so you can put each one down and move on to the next name efficiently.

3. Once it's been a minute or two and you can't think of anyone else you know, set the intention with your superconscious to help you sort out which of these people you think could support you in using the full authority of your authentic self, moving forward on your unitary path, and pursuing your calling. Circle the names of those you think might be able to support you; cross out the names of those you think will not. Don't circle the names of people who might give you good advice and challenge you

but not really support you. Only circle the names of people who will support you—challenges will come later.

4. Once you are done with the circling and crossing out, go over your list. Do you have at least one name circled? If so, go to step 6.

5. If you don't have at least one name circled, go to step 2 and keep brainstorming names. Consider the folks in your gym, your neighbor who smiles at you every so often—look far and wide. If you are stymied, go to this book's website at http://www. thecallingprogram.com and look for the "calling circle" page, which will tell you where you can find others around the world who are interested in being in a calling circle.

6. Looking at the names you circled, ask yourself of each one, "Can I support this person in using the full authority of their authentic self, maintaining a unitary path, and working toward their calling?" If so, mark that person's name with a star. If you end up with no starred names on your list, go to step 5.

7. When you have at least one name that is both circled and starred, you are done. You will need this list later in this chapter (see "Introducing Your Calling Circle to Itself").

Once you've completed this exercise, step back and check in with yourself. How do you feel? You might have noticed that this exercise can bring up difficult feelings. You might have found yourself crossing off, or just not starring, names that you feel "should" be on the list for your calling circle. Your spouse, parents, children, siblings, coworkers…it's almost guaranteed that you will feel that at least one of these people is not appropriate for your calling circle. That could be because they are too challenging for you. Or it could be because you know they won't support your authentic self or your calling, or that you can't support theirs, or that their role in your life is not appropriate to be in your calling circle.

Some people will avoid doing this exercise to stay away from the feelings of disappointment and anger that can arise from recognizing that at least some people don't feel supportive. That makes sense. But creating a calling circle is essential, so let's take a moment to talk about this anger you might have about people in your life not feeling connected to or supportive of you or your calling.

Anger: Missing Connection and Support

It's totally reasonable to feel angry about the sludge that has managed to separate you from your calling in the past. Largely consisting of messages from your family, friends, community, and even yourself, the sludge may have covered over your calling for a really long time. The lack of support around us is practically an epidemic, and anger can be very helpful in breaking through to the other side, where support can be more easily felt.

Insight: Anger brings us the gift of connection to ourselves, but only when we feel the anger and let it go.

It's useful to distinguish two types of anger that can help us connect to ourselves, and they behave in different ways. *Motivational anger*, the kind of anger that allows you to power through barriers, is exemplified by a friend of mine who lived for a time in a battered-women's shelter. She had been physically abused by her husband, who told her that if she sought help he would go after her. She was afraid, hurt, and especially angry. Her husband's threat—a severe and tangible one—became a block that prevented her action. Fortunately, over time this threat stimulated motivational anger that prompted her to look for other options. She told me that one day she woke up realizing that her husband couldn't hurt her if he didn't have access to her. She called a shelter with twenty-four-hour security in another town and moved there the next week. Her motivational anger allowed her to break through to a place where support was available.

There's also *protective anger*—the kind that is designed to keep us from being hurt by the everyday ups and downs of life. This type of anger is more chronic. For instance, one client I coached was perpetually angry. She would lash out at anyone in her path. Whenever we talked, she would tell me a different story about why she was angry: someone was incompetent at work, there was an infantile discussion on a radio talk show, she was overlooked for a promotion. But upon closer inspection, her stories were always the same: they were about her perception that she was not being allowed to act in the world, that there was always someone or something preventing her from pursuing her calling. My sense was that her anger was protecting her from seeing both her fear about acting in the world and her sadness about not connecting with others. Ultimately, I had to terminate our coaching sessions and refer her to a therapist, because I couldn't help her with her protective anger. At that point, she lashed out at me. This could have been justified—she needed a therapist, and I was a coach, and maybe she felt that I should have been a therapist. But, in any case, her anger at me seemed to be protecting her from experiencing her own, more difficult feelings, like fear and sadness. The strange thing about protective anger is that, in the end, it doesn't help; it keeps us away from a potential source of healing— honest connections with other human beings.

My friend in the abusive relationship felt that her motivational anger was useful in that it drove her to change her environment. Her anger built up until it could break through her own inability to think of alternatives to her situation. Afterward, over time, her anger was released, and she could begin to heal. In contrast, the protective, chronic kind of anger my former client exemplified never seems to overtake anything; it digs a deeper trench between ourselves and others. Although most of us have experienced both types of anger, it's good to know the difference. Motivational anger helps us push through a block and create change; protective anger keeps things from changing. Acknowledging both, when either one is present, connects us to ourselves.

Once you have diagnosed your anger, you can use it appropriately. You can use motivational anger to overcome blocks, and you can use protective anger to discover what the more vulnerable parts of you want to avoid changing. The problem is that you can't always tell the difference between these two kinds of anger when you're simply feeling angry. So one way to move forward with undiagnosed anger is to treat all anger the same way until your anger starts to behave as one form or the other. By their differences you'll know how to use them.

Here's an example: Your partner leaves the bath mat on the floor, and you get annoyed because you feel like they are taking your natural neatness for granted; you feel like you're the one who always has to tidy up. You pick up the bath mat and tell your partner how you feel. After your initial burst of anger, you find it easy to work with your partner to reach a compromise that suits you both. You are able to move forward without another thought. Once your anger is released and you have used it to change your situation, you can see that it was motivational anger.

Another way it could go: Your partner leaves the bath mat on the floor, and you get really angry because you feel like they are taking your natural neatness for granted. You pick up the bath mat and talk with your partner, telling them you're the one who has to tidy up and you don't like it. You are unable to accept any of their explanations, and you can't seem to come to a useful compromise. You are still angry as you leave the conversation. Your inability to reach a compromise with your partner or to let your anger release itself tells you that this anger is probably protecting something deeper. You discover that you have a feeling that if you get close to your partner, you will be taken for granted, but you also realize that you haven't shared your wishes about the bath mat with your partner. You see that your anger seems to be something that protects you from getting close and sharing the truth about your wishes with your partner. You discuss this with your partner, who totally understands and announces a wish for you to share more about what you want to happen around the house. Your anger begins to dissolve and, as a nice bonus, the bath mat is no longer left on the floor!

Both types of anger are okay, and both need to be experienced and released when they arise. Unfortunately, many cultural forces tell us that anger is a problem, so you may not have been taught how to experience and then let go of anger. That's fine, we'll fix that! Here's an exercise that helps you experience and release your anger.

Brief Exercise

This activity is a lot of fun—you get to throw a fit, on purpose.
What you'll need:

- Fifteen minutes alone in a fairly empty, private space with nothing living in it (plants, animals, or other people), a place where you won't mind making loud and possibly embarrassing noises

- A safe and unbreakable tool for your anger—a punching bag, a pillow, a rage doll

- Your lab notebook

1. Go to your private space, bringing your anger tool. In this space, you will let your anger move through you.

2. Gather all your anger. Imagine anything or anyone that blocks your path. Imagine them right in front of you, and feel your anger pushing at these blocks.

3. Now—even if you don't feel angry—move or dance as hard as you can. Scream, yell, announce whatever anger you feel to the

world with your body and your voice. If you have the urge to hit something, make sure it's with your anger tool, not your bare hands or feet.

4. Keep on moving and making noise as you feel your anger rise up within you. If your anger starts to slow down or turn into something else, it's likely motivational; go to step 5 to work with it. If your anger keeps coming through you for ten or more minutes, it's probably protective; go to step 6 to work with it.

5. Use this step for motivational anger: Notice exactly what your anger has become; this is the power behind your anger, and it's yours to use. Dance and move with your new feelings. Let yourself look back at your blocks and discover whether you have any further insights about what they were and why they were there. Write these insights in your notebook.

6. Use this step for protective anger: Slow down your anger voluntarily by slowing your movements and quieting your voice. As you do, start to dance and move with the intention of letting your superconscious show you what part of you feels afraid and vulnerable. Through noticing your movements, take a guess at what this part is. Write your insights in your notebook. Then, ask your superconscious if there is one practical thing you can do to begin giving yourself what you need to help support this part. Make a commitment to do this, if you can.

Experiencing and releasing anger is an excellent practice. It can actually be fun to see what the anger is trying to tell you. It's like communicating with a whole new part of yourself. And then there's the "makeup sex," whether that's with yourself or someone else—it's a delight to reconnect so deliciously!

Okay, after taking a nice break for that makeup sex, let's return to preparing your calling circle so that it's healthy, strong, and ready for you to claim your calling publicly. The next step is introducing your calling circle—to itself!

Introducing Your Calling Circle to Itself

Thanks to the calling circle exercise you completed earlier in this chapter, you now have a list of at least one other person, potentially more, who is a good candidate for your calling circle. Now comes the time when you ask at least one of the people on your list to be in your calling circle. Remember that a calling circle is nothing more than you and all the people you've chosen to be part of the circle, one on one, supporting each other. It is not a major time commitment, and no group meetings are necessary—unless that's something you want. It is you working with each of the people you've picked for your calling circle to work toward your callings. And keep in mind that you're the only one who has to know all the people who are in your circle. You're not asking them to hang out together; they don't even need to know who else is in your circle. You're asking them to be supportive of you, and you're asking yourself to be supportive of them.

> **Insight:** The act of asking for unconditional support of who you are, in itself, will create a safe space in which you can begin to pursue your calling.

Even after all these caveats, asking people to support you in this work can feel terrifying. But it's important to remind yourself that the only way to get through these next four weeks is to know that there are other people who have explicitly agreed to support you in your calling.

The process of asking people to be in your calling circle is one really great way to eventually discover some of your shortcomings and also some of your gifts. When we are operating within ourselves, in our own worlds, we know how to play down both our areas of genius and our character flaws. But trying to support even just one other person while also simultaneously trying to be supported by that person requires us to grapple with the wholeness of who we are in a way that we just cannot do on our own.

Brief Exercise

In this exercise, you're going to ask people on your list to be in your calling circle. Let's walk through it and see what happens.

1. Get out your lab notebook and welcome yourself into your inner lab. Bring your phone or computer—some way to communicate with people on your list.

2. Set the intention with your superconscious that you will have brief but clear conversations with each person you're considering for your calling circle. Also set the intention that you will be safe and well taken care of in these conversations. Assure your superconsicous that if at any point you do not feel safe and well taken care of, you will either tell the other person or end the conversation as quickly and kindly as possible.

3. Looking at your list of potential calling circle members in your lab notebook, think about contacting one. How do you feel? Write down how you feel.

4. Contact that person. Let them know that you're working on getting really clear about your true work in the world and that you're hoping they can support you in that process and be authentic with you, as you will try to be with them. If they agree, let them know you might turn to them every so often to discuss different ideas and decisions with them. And invite them to do that with you as well. You might tell them you want support, not necessarily advice. No need to tell them yet what your calling is—you're looking for unconditional support that doesn't rely on them approving of or commenting on your calling ahead of time (you will tell them your calling later this week when you do the Activating Your Calling Circle experiment).

5. After that conversation is over (or after the email or voicemail is sent) check in with yourself and write down in your lab notebook how you feel.

6. Do steps 3 through 5 until all potential members of your calling circle are contacted.

Nicely done! You have asked at least one person to be in your calling circle. Don't worry if they say they can't do it right now or it's not for them. Keep trying—if you set the intention with your superconscious to help you find someone who is right for your calling circle, it will happen.

Activating Your Calling Circle

The world at large does not make it easy to feel continuously connected to your authenticity and authority, or to understand and pursue your calling. There are forces that would like us to give up our own power in the world. Sometimes these forces are cultural, such as expectations that certain groups of people—women, minorities, disabled people—will be passive. Other times the forces are within ourselves, such as the fears that arise when we contemplate the responsibility power brings.

If you find yourself giving up or not claiming your power in the world, you can draw on your calling circle to get back in touch with your authority and back on the path of your true work. For the final bit of work this week, we'll use an experiment to look into how it feels to begin using your calling circle as support.

⚗ Activating Your Calling Circle

Goal: To discuss your calling with the person or people in your circle and see how that feels.

Time required: 15–20 minutes

This experiment is about saying your calling out loud to the people in your calling circle, asking for their reactions, then practicing listening carefully to their descriptions of their true work (to the extent they want to share their callings with you). Be prepared for a complete lack of surprise on their part—the people in your calling circle probably have a better sense of your calling than you do, and they may anticipate your calling. Also expect lots of supportive words as well as some misunderstandings. The more your calling is out there and out loud in the world, and the more capable you are of listening to feedback about it, the freer you will be to pursue it without drama.

1. Visualize the boundaries of your authority.

    Mentally draw a boundary around your inner lab and place yourself firmly inside the boundary. In this experiment, it's important to speak from your inner lab, because it is the place from which your authority arises. Visualize yourself speaking about your calling while you remain firmly in this inner laboratory.

2. Choose one person to tell.

    With your whole self, pick a person in your calling circle, and choose a way to tell them your calling. Select a method you can use right now that gives immediate feedback, not something like, "When I see that person next month, I'll tell her" or "I can text my friend about it." In other words, choose a face-to-face meeting, a teleconference, or phone call. When you tell this person your calling, what you are going to bring into the world, it will be a sacred moment. Treat it as such. Ask them to listen until you are done.

3. Share your calling.

    While visualizing yourself standing firmly within the boundaries of your authority, and therefore acknowledging that you have no control over other people's responses, share your calling. Challenge yourself to not use any caveats like, "It may sound weird, but..." Just tell this person or multiple people what your calling is, in the plainest terms. Ask the person to repeat your calling back to you. Then ask for their feedback about how your calling feels to them. Still standing firmly in your inner laboratory, carefully observe the response you get.

4. Listen for their calling.

    When you are done sharing about your calling, ask if they have a sense of their calling; if yes, ask them how they would phrase it. Promise them that you'll consider their response seriously and supportively.

5. Record how that felt.

    Write down in your lab notebook your experience of steps 1 through 4. What happened? Did any of your shortcomings show themselves to you? Any new gifts of your own to appreciate?

6. Consider telling the world.

    Think about telling more people. If you have others in your calling circle, consider telling them—start back at step 1. If you want, consider posting your first-pass definition of your calling on the website for this book: http://www.thecallingprogram.com /mycalling. After you are all done, write down in your lab notebook what you experienced in this experiment and what shortcomings or gifts, if any, became apparent to you.

Remember that your calling circle will evolve with time; it will grow and shrink as people enter and leave it naturally. Whenever you're in an authentic state, look around and see to whom you're attracted as a human being. Then reach out to them. They may withdraw or they may come close. Learning how to talk with other people while staying true to your calling is really important right now. At the beginning of this work, in part I, you listened from your inner lab. Now you're learning to speak to others from your inner lab.

Conclusion

This was a preparation-intensive week, but necessarily so. Having your calling circle in place gives you the base from which you can energize your calling. You've got the beginnings of your team.

It's a big deal to work through the anger and fear that almost all of us have about sharing with others our important work in the world. You've done well, but it's not over yet. This work will continue next week, as you experiment with trusting yourself and others more fully.

Experimenting with Trust

Objective: To increase your sense of trust as a result of practicing boundaries, understanding your responsibilities, and using discernment.

Why Trust?

If beginning to create your calling circle has already energized you, you might be feeling impatient and ready to move on. You've got your people, you're ready to go! But the whole point of this part of the program is to take the time it takes to energize your calling, and you do this at least partially by learning from your team. The fastest way to learn from a team of people is to try to trust them and see what happens.

If you don't try trusting your calling circle, you can't make progress. You will have a team of people who aren't really being useful. On the other hand, if you do try trusting them, you'll learn a lot about yourself in general and a lot about your shortcomings—and theirs—in particular.

As a result of the necessity of trusting your calling circle, you might have guessed that the crucial experiment this week is all about trust. Before we get there, we need to talk about how trust works.

How Trust Works

Most of us think of trust in ourselves and trust in others as two different things. I have many colleagues who would rather do everything themselves than trust anyone else to do it correctly. They would say that's because they trust themselves but not others.

But that doesn't make complete sense. If someone really trusts themselves, that means they trust that they will pick the right colleagues to work with and trust that they will communicate effectively with those colleagues about work. So when someone claims they only trust themselves, what they mean is that they trust no one, not even themselves.

> **Insight:** Trust always goes both ways. If you trust yourself, it's easy to trust others. If others trust you, it's because you trust yourself.

Trust goes both ways—it's like it is something we access rather than something we own. If you own something, it's exclusively yours. If you access it, there's no limit to the number of people who can tap in and use it. To speak more to the power of accessing trust, meet Eddie.

Eddie: The Power of Trust

Eddie* is the founder of a cybersecurity company, built on the idea that trust is powerful and that mutual trust can be grown and nurtured. The idea is inherent in the culture of the company: each person is responsible for her or his own project assignments, with explicit conversations about expectations, results, and how to maintain effective mutual workflows. This is not only explicitly stated, but it is also supported through company-wide transparency, individual mentorship, and explicit declarations of support for each individual's authenticity and authority. The culture of trust so pervades *the company that it naturally flows through to its interactions with other companies, ever increasing the circle of trust.*

When I asked Eddie how he would describe his calling, he said, "Over time I discovered that I love taking complex things and finding ways to make them simple. I discover and share insights that explicate the core of a system without trivializing or negating the thing itself. I joke that my gift is being able to dumb stuff down." He offered as an example a talk that he had given on artificial intelligence. He has given that talk to a wide variety of audiences, and both novices and experts have come up to him afterwards and said they now had insights they'd never had before. When I asked Eddie to describe the path by which he discovered this calling, he told me a story that shows the humility that emerges from accessing trust.

Eddie told me, "There were times in the history of our company when the relationships among the employees I was managing were not going well. I kept trying to fix it, but I was driving myself too hard and I had lost clarity in my own mind about what was needed for the company. I had an overwhelming sense of confusion. I couldn't see anything. I had put my heart and soul into this company and I could see it was in danger of being destroyed. Yet I couldn't fix it."

At the end of his rope, Eddie's coach Kelly told him that he needed to remove himself from the situation; he needed to go home until he came through this. It was a gut-wrenching decision, but he did it. Eddie's level of trust in Kelly was so complete that he told the company he was taking a sabbatical and left that same day. "I surrendered completely because of my trust in her. She has a profound spiritual sense." His sabbatical ended up being six months, after which he was able to return and start the restructuring work that was needed.

When I heard this, I dug further—how did Eddie, who said he felt he needed to solve everything, get to the point where he felt he could trust his coach Kelly? It turns out that this story also began with trust. Eddie had a business friend who suggested inviting Kelly to a planning meeting as a management consultant. That meeting was the first time Eddie met his future coach.

Eddie recalls, "I hadn't ever been impressed by management consultants in the past, but I didn't mind her sitting in. Kelly sat at the back. At the end of the meeting she asked if she could make a few comments. 'Sure,' I said, so she started sharing her observations. 'Remember when you were talking with Alan, and you said this, he said that, and the conversation went off track?' I did remember. She continued, 'This is what was happening,' and she diagnosed our communication breakdown with complete clarity and simplicity! Her insight was astounding! I realized it was same thing I can do for ideas, but she did it for something interpersonal."

Eddie knew he needed someone like that in his circle. He could also see that Kelly's calling was coherent with his own, just applied to a different field. As a closing thought, Eddie pointed out, "It required humility to admit I needed anyone at all." Trust led to more trust, which led to healing and repair, which led to more insight.

Eddie's insight that humility was necessary for him to recognize he might need someone is key. Humility also helped him see his own gifts, reflected in someone else. But wait— weren't we talking about trust? Well, trust and humility are related. Feeling humble is another way of saying that you feel safe and protected because you have trust for yourself and those around you. Humility is an outgrowth of trust. When you access trust, you can allow other people to give you feedback and help you in your work.

Insight: Trusting yourself and others allows you to change in ways that energize your calling.

Another way to understand the power of trust is to look at what would have happened to Eddie's company if he didn't have it. He would never have accepted Kelly (an outsider) at his meeting, he would not have been open to her deep coaching, he would have assumed that he needed to solve the interpersonal problems that were breaking apart his company, and his company would likely have disintegrated. Instead, he and his company learned from their mistakes, became energized, and are thriving today, thanks to the power of trust.

The Cost of Not Trusting Yourself

So here we are together, experimenting with trusting ourselves enough to actually be in relationships with the people in our calling circles and all the people we will need to work with to help our callings come to life. In a way, trusting yourself is scarier than attempting to trust others, because it's the core of trust. If you can't trust yourself to stand up for yourself, there's no way to trust others. They will always violate your trust, because it's pre-violated by you. You will be in the habit of not giving others the very information they need to earn your trust—specifically, what is and isn't okay with you within the boundaries of your relationships.

Not trusting myself has caused difficulties in my work more than once. For instance, I'm leading a technology startup where we work intensively on solving problems. As the leader, I've often felt that my job is to solve all problems. It's a pattern that's played out in any number of contexts in which I have had a leadership role. In those situations, I didn't express this obligation aloud or say anything about it bothering me, because I made the assumption that, in exchange for leading, my desires needed to be sacrificed for the good of the team. Over time, a negative feedback loop developed, and I started to resent the people with whom I worked because they would refer their problems to me. I began to feel that I couldn't trust them to take care of me—a feeling I now realize is inappropriate. Because taking care of me is not their job. It's mine.

Here's how that dynamic ended up crashing and burning at my startup one particular week. Because I believed I was the one who had to solve all the problems, I was worried about how I would solve a funding problem. So I hurried into a solution—I decided to meet with an investor and talk with him about what we hoped to achieve—even though I had been told by our advisory team that it was too early to contact investors. But, the thing was, I felt that I had to solve this problem. So I went ahead and contacted the investor.

My business advisers were connected with this investor, and when I told them about the meeting, they knew I had jumped the gun. Then they felt uncomfortable with the investor, because they were supposed to be giving me and our team advice about how to do these things. They told me about their annoyance at my behavior, and I went into a shame spiral. Why did I just go ahead and try to solve the funding problem alone?

When I turned to them to ask what they wanted in the future, the advisory team said, *"Please, Julia, please* let us help you." Even though I believed I trusted myself enough to cultivate good advisers, they pointed out that I hadn't been asking for advice. And it was true. Here they were, much more knowledgeable about the business world than I was, but I was proceeding instead as though I had to do everything myself. I saw that my assumption that I needed to solve everything myself was not only wrong, and it not only smacked of lack of trust, it would cause major problems for my calling if I didn't correct it.

It can be a difficult process, recognizing and repairing your own lack of trust. It would be nice if there was another option. It may seem that another option would be crawling under a rock and refusing to work with other people. But the fact is, your calling can't work without the help of others. Even if your calling is to see how many rocks you can crawl under, you still need someone to bring you lunch while you're under all those rocks. So the best option I know is to learn to access trust—for yourself and others. To access trust, you'll have to decide what your deal-breakers are.

Deal-Breakers and Deal-Makers

Trusting yourself to take care of yourself means that you will let people on your team—in your calling circle and hopefully beyond—know whenever something won't work for you. Whatever won't work for you is your deal-breaker. What is a deal-breaker? Something that, if it happened, would make you consider cutting off your relationship with someone else. Sure, you get extra credit for telling other people what you dislike—for instance, I tell my team I don't like them using the word "guys" to refer to mixed-gender groups that contain women. But some of them still do it. I've said what I needed to say, they've listened, and it's not a deal-breaker.

> **Insight:** When you tell people how they can succeed in being in a relationship with you, you can access trust.

My deal-breakers are not respecting my body and its personal space, cruelty, and not respecting my intelligence and agency. If someone violates them, I know I have to do three things to continue to trust myself. First, I have to try to get away from the situation so I can think about what to do. Then, at some point I need to decide if I want to tell the other person that what they did wasn't okay with me. Finally, I need to choose whether that person will be in my life or not.

To experiment with trust is to bring the full authority of your authentic self and your unitary path forward to their logical evolution. If you are using the full authority of your authentic self and you want only to move forward on a single, unitary path, you must be clear about your deal-breakers in your relationships. Otherwise, you're pretending that your deal-breakers don't exist, which violates the authority of your authentic self, or you're pretending that your path doesn't matter, which violates the unitarity of your path. Clearly, your deal-breakers are very important. But so are your deal-makers—the things that you would like people in your life to do. Let's figure out what both of them are.

Brief Exercise

In this exercise, you'll discover your deal-breakers as well as your deal-makers; these create the boundaries that will help you learn to trust yourself as you pursue relationships that energize your calling.

1. Get your lab notebook out.

2. Go into your inner lab. Just as a reminder of your authority, imagine a sphere around your body. This is your zone of influence—where your authority lives. Fill it with love. You live here, and it is a loving place.

3. Once you feel full of love for yourself, open your lab notebook and make two columns. Label one "Deal-makers: What people can do around me" and the other "Deal-breakers: What people can't do around me."

4. You can start in either column, but each time you write something down, put a related action in the other column. So if you write "give me consensual hugs," "give me constructive criticism," and "tell stories about drinking" in the "What people can do around me" column, you might put "uninvited touch," "criticize anyone based on race or gender," and "tell stories about sex" in the "deal-breakers" column. These are just examples; the contents of your two columns will be unique to you.

5. Give yourself about ten minutes to finish up.

6. Take a look at your lists. You'll notice that certain themes emerge that naturally suggest a few overarching deal-breakers, like "cruelty of any type." Write those down at the bottom of the page. "My deal-breakers are: _____." Look at your deal-makers, and include the overarching themes, like "kindness." Write those down at the bottom of the page. "My deal-makers are: _____."

7. Follow those with a commitment to yourself: "I trust myself to communicate my deal-makers and deal-breakers to the people

in my life, try my best to leave the situation if any of my boundaries are violated, assess whether to tell the offending party, and consciously choose whether to keep this person in my life."

By getting clarity on your deal-makers and your deal-breakers, you're beginning to access trust. Why? Because now you and others have a chance to do right by you. You're taking care of yourself, so that's no longer on other people's shoulders. Perhaps, paradoxically, you will feel more cared for.

Dividing Responsibilities to Make Trust Work for You

The strengthening of relationships that results from trust can only come when you are clear about whose job is whose when it comes to trust. To help figure this out, let's list the jobs. To access trust fully, you need to really understand the list of things your authentic self is responsible for in your relationships. This list includes:

- Deciding both *with whom* and *when* you start, maintain, and end relationships

- Making your deal-breakers clear to others

- Making your deal-makers clear to others

- Getting away from people when they violate a deal-breaker, if at all possible

- Deciding whether to remain in relationships with people who have violated your deal-breakers

- Unraveling the damage to yourself, your relationships, and others that is done if you don't take responsibility for the above

There is only one thing your authentic self is *not* responsible for in your relationships. But it's a big thing: *Anything that other people do at any time, as long as you are taking responsibility for items 1 through 5 above.* This includes the feelings and behaviors of other people after you have made your boundaries clear, the feelings and behaviors of other people that follow after you have apologized and taken responsibility for any damage you've caused by not making your boundaries clear, and any feelings or behaviors of any other people that arise for any other reason.

Does that feel like a relief? It should. Together with the tools of using the full authority of your authentic self and moving forward on a unitary path, accessing trust again brings your focus back to you. It's a relief when we realize the truth: not only can we not fix others, we are only able to change ourselves when we stop trying to worry about everyone else.

The Importance of Discernment

Once you begin to access trust and divide up the jobs in your relationships, the importance of discernment about what is done and said becomes clear. What is done and said by others you trust, even if you trust them completely, is not necessarily right. Remember way back in Week 1 when we had the insight, "Just because you have a strong intuition doesn't mean it's right, and if you only have a weak intuition, that doesn't mean it's wrong"? We can apply that insight to trust.

Insight: Just because you trust someone doesn't mean their advice is right, and if you don't trust someone, that doesn't mean their advice is wrong.

The critical adjunct to trust is discernment, which can be restated as trusting yourself to know the right next step when you hear it. You can think of discernment as a steering wheel that guides you on your unitary path. It requires trust of both others and yourself. You access trust of others to be available to other people, to be open to hearing their insights about you and what's next for your calling. And then you access trust of yourself—your discernment—to choose what you will do and how you'll do it.

This interplay between trust of others and trust of yourself is exactly the same as the necessary dance between intuitions about how things might work and actual, real-world experiments that tell you how things work. You need both, and each one informs the other, in an endless chain. Your intuitions get better as more experimental results come in, and your experiments become more successful as your intuitions improve. In essence, this endless chain of trust of self and trust of others represents the underlying mechanics of how you will engage your calling in the world. You will keep going from trusting others to discernment to trusting others to discernment again. It won't let up but, fortunately, it will get much easier and way more fun.

Trusting Your Calling Circle

An understanding of the power of trust and the importance of discernment would not be complete without putting this understanding into practice. So the final piece of work this week is doing just that. You'll practice trusting the others in your calling circle.

⚗ The Trust Experiment

Goal: To use trust to further understand the next steps for how you will pursue your calling.

Time required: 15 minutes to several hours, depending on what emerges

The plan for this experiment is to choose one person in your calling circle to trust, ask them what they think your next step is toward pursuing your calling, take that step to a second person in your circle, build on it, and see what happens. You're letting your calling circle in. It's now safe to do that—you have learned to access trust.

1. Review your boundaries.

    Get out your lab notebook and review your deal-makers and deal-breakers.

2. Choose your experimental subject.

    Go into your inner lab and summon the full authority of your authentic self. Let someone in your calling circle come to mind. This is your experimental subject. You'll practice trusting them. Contact them and ask for an appointment to talk for five to ten minutes. Don't start the appointment until you read the next step.

3. Be in a place of humility.

    Just before the time comes to talk with your experimental subject, put yourself in a place of humility by reminding yourself what you are responsible for in your relationships (the lists above). You're going to get feedback about what you need to do next, and, by trusting yourself, you can be ready to hear anything this person has to tell you. Once you're ready and it's time for your appointment, remind your experimental subject of what your calling is, and ask them what they intuitively think your next step might be. If they are not sure, tell them that's okay, that they can just choose whatever comes to mind.

4. Listen and thank them.

    Listen carefully, repeating what you think they said to see if you got it right. Then thank them for their help and write down in your lab notebook what they said your next step might be.

5. Discern whether you will take that step.

    Imagine yourself moving forward on your unitary path. Does it feel right for you to do the step they are suggesting? Does it feel like there might be some merit to it? If so, write down in your lab notebook how you will do it and by what date you commit to doing it. If the step does not feel right, write down in your lab notebook another, related step that is close in meaning to the one suggested by your experimental subject. Also write down the date by which you will have completed that step. For instance, if the experimental subject tells you that your next step is to enroll in a dance class, but your knees make that impossible, you might instead write down when you will enroll in a drumming class. Notice that regardless of whether the step felt right or not, your interaction with your experimental subject moved you closer to energizing your calling by giving you a next step to consider. Write down how it feels to have your steps influenced by others.

6. Ask at least one more calling circle member.

   Go back and do steps 2 through 5 again, this time taking your next step with you. Ask advice on how to hone this step, and listen carefully to any advice you receive. Once you arrive at step 5, in your lab notebook, write down any new insights about or changes in your next step. If the step has changed, write down a new version of your commitment to do the step.

7. Do the step you committed to do.

   By the end of this week, do the step you committed to do in step 5. Write down how it feels when you accomplish that step and the outcome of it. Record whether you feel the step energizes your calling.

8. Be available. Make sure the others in your unfolding circle know that you are available as experimental subjects for their trust experiments.

Most of us do this kind of thing casually. We talk with a friend to ask advice, then talk with another to check out the advice. You can do less formal versions of this experiment for the rest of your life; as long as you access trust as you do it, you'll get excellent results.

Conclusion

This week, you arranged things so that you could taste the experience of accessing trust, including understanding boundaries, responsibilities, and discernment. At this point, you're halfway through the Calling program.

Next week you'll kick the energizing of your calling into high gear by experimenting with love. You'll experience accepting and actively loving your shortcomings as well as the shortcomings of others. You started working with love a bit this week when you filled your inner lab with love, but next week will be a full-blown lovefest, so get ready.

Experimenting with Love

Objective: To become more aware of your major shortcomings and actively love them, while simultaneously loving the shortcomings of your calling circle and your calling itself.

Two Kinds of Love

The word "love" can set people off on the wrong foot, especially in a professional context. This is probably because they are thinking of the kind of love the Greeks called "eros," which is thought to suggest sexual love. Meanwhile, "agape," another Greek word for love, is thought to reference sacred love. Mentioning sex or religion in a professional context can be tricky, so most people veer away from talking about love all together, at least at work.

These definitions of eros and agape are a bit old fashioned, but modern-day philosophers have updated them (e.g., Crabtree 2017). Regardless, in this book "love" means *agape*—in its updated meaning of *unconditional love*. This is love that allows the lover to fully and benevolently accept the one who is loved.

Like trust, this kind of love is not owned by anyone—it is simply accessed by anyone who feels it. And, like trust, it arises simultaneously in the lover and the loved. The loved one could be another person, an idea, an animal, and so on. If you have unconditional love for yourself, you are both the lover and the loved.

For us to have unconditional love of anyone, we must love ourselves. "In fact, we *must* exercise agapic love towards ourselves. We cannot exclude any creature—including ourselves—from that love… Rather than viewing our duty to love ourselves as objectionable, agape emphasizes its central role in evolutionary growth" (Crabtree 2017, 39, italics mine).

Insight: To access unconditional love, you must love yourself.

Most of us can say we love ourselves sometimes—but not all the time. This week you will aim toward "all the time." You will work on becoming keenly aware of your own shortcomings and loving each one, in turn. Once you do that for yourself, you will become aware of and love the shortcomings of your calling circle and your calling itself.

If you're asking why this kind of radical self- and other-love is necessary in order to energize your calling, the answer is that without experimenting with love—without turning on your "love light," so to speak—you won't get very far when you work on engaging your calling (you'll get to this in part III). If trust and discernment are like a steering wheel, love is your engine. Without trust and disconcerment, you can't steer. Without love, you won't go anywhere.

Don't believe me? Soon you'll try the experiment yourself to see if it works. But before you do, it's worth looking at how Maureen used love to help her move forward on her unitary path, when she was in clear danger of stalling out.

Maureen: Using Love to Move Mountains

Maureen was in her fifties when I interviewed her. A feminist social worker with decades of experience in helping people shift their paradigms to new ones that serve them better, Maureen serves on multiple nonprofit boards focused on making the cultural changes that she sees as necessary for the world. I asked her if she had an early memory of connecting to her calling, and she told me about a time when she was five years old and had a complex set of feelings about her place in the world.

"I had this profound sense of caring and compassion for other life forms: earth, animals, people. I remember passionately learning the St. Francis prayer ('make me a channel of your peace')—I was raised Catholic—and really resonating with it and praying it as if I had found a touchstone on the planet. I was kneeling by my bed when I had this deep sense of my ability to care, which is a blessing and a curse. The other piece was how lonely I felt. It was a deep connection to something bigger than myself, and knowing it, and also being aware of where I was—on Earth—and how disconnected people were around me."

I asked Maureen what her calling is, and she told me it is "to allow joy to create through me. Joy is a state of playfulness. Inquisitiveness and curiousness. Aliveness. When I wake up in the morning, I say to myself, 'How do I create with my joy today?' Then I go into the world and I might be able to express my anger clearly at an injustice or compassionately care about someone's suffering, but there's joy in it. The joy is the essence of it."

Her calling sounded so global that I wondered if she ever felt as if she wasn't doing that, and, if so, how she got back on her path. Her answer is where Maureen's story of using love to get her calling to move forward emerged.

"There was a time in my life when I became involved with my husband, and an entire community led by his family and ex-wife vilified and attacked me. I lost my bearings. The irony is that they were witch-hunting me because of my aliveness, my joy. How did I get back on the path? I had to go through the pain and the suffering of being vilified by the court of public opinion. I had to see my powerlessness in the situation and basically rise above it, knowing that none of it had

anything to do with me; it was just their stuff getting projected onto me. And I had to have compassion for them. I did a lot of loving-kindness meditation [metta meditation] and found my way back to my joy and my truth. I let them be who they are, suffer the way they chose, but I developed really good boundaries because of their behavior. I then became stronger in being connected to myself, my joy, and my spiritual being in this physical form."

Maureen was in a dark place, and she knew that the only way forward was through—through feeling everything, then loving everything—including herself and her tormenters. I asked her what message she would give to her five-year-old self, and she said, "It's such a gift to be so caring. Caring is kindness, compassion, and action—which involves knowing what is and setting really good boundaries, so that you don't take on other people's suffering."

Maureen clearly uses the tools of trust and love to energize her calling, and her success at what she does is evidence that these tools work. You've got trust under your belt. Let's move on to allowing love to work for you.

Loving Yourself

Whether you can say you love yourself might depend on how you define "yourself." If you include in "yourself" only the parts of you that you think are lovable, then yes, you can love yourself without too much trouble. But unless you consider every single part of yourself lovable—including your shortcomings—you are ignoring important parts of your authentic self. These parts are not getting love. Loving only the lovable parts is not agapic, unconditional love—it is loving under the condition that the loved one is pre-screened for only the good bits! Meanwhile, we are playing with the idea that the engine that drives your calling is *unconditional* love.

Before we go further, let's talk briefly about unconditional love. Many people get concerned about practicing unconditional love. The overarching fear seems to be that if dark, negative, or wrong-thinking parts of ourselves are loved, they will grow in size and take over. If this were true, the obvious solution would be to make sure not to love them. It only makes sense. But the key point here is that this fear is not true. When you love dark, negative, or wrong-thinking parts of yourself, they begin to become transformed into something that is light, positive, and right-thinking. We'll practice this now in a brief exercise, so you can experience this yourself.

Brief Exercise

We'll work with judgments because they're generally considered to be wrong-thinking or dark parts of ourselves. At the same time, almost everyone has them, so you can usually find at least one judgment to use for this exercise.

1. Get your lab notebook and scan your memory of the last week, noticing and writing down a judgment that you had about someone else. Put the judgment in a simple sentence, like this: "My boss doesn't respond to emails, even when I'm trying to help her. That's irresponsible."

2. Now take the sentence and rework it so it starts this way: "I wish I could get away with _____." For the example in step 1, your reworked sentence might be, "I wish I could get away with not responding to emails and being irresponsible."

3. Then take a moment to feel the truth of that statement. Now see how you might feel if you actually could get away with what you were judging the other person for. Write, "It would make me feel _____." For the example above you might write, "It would make me feel free."

4. Notice that your lack of love for the other person was based on a part of yourself that you didn't feel was lovable—the part that wishes it could get away with what the other person is actually getting away with. Give that part of yourself a name. For the example above it might be called "my happy-go-lucky child-part."

5. Now go into your inner lab and find a chair to sit in—find one you really like. Sit that newly named part of yourself in a chair opposite yours, and give it a really nice chair—the kind of chair it would like. Now tell that part of yourself that you love it and that you understand its desire to be with you and included in the parts that are loved. If you don't feel honest as you say this, listen a bit to what this part has to say and what it needs from you. Then try again until you can feel the love coming through you for this part sitting opposite you.

6. Write down in your lab notebook how that went for you, and take a moment to reread your original judgment, the one you wrote in step 1. How do you feel now about the person you had judged? Has your judgment grown or shrunk?

This brief exercise is doubly useful. First, it shows you the link between unconditional love for all parts of yourself and unconditional love for others. Second, the exercise points out that by loving parts of yourself that you previously thought were bad or wrong-thinking, you learn what they are trying to tell you and can then love them. In the process of loving them, you transform these parts into helpful allies that remind you of important truths that you might otherwise have forgotten. In this example, the person who wanted the freedom of irresponsibility will now have a happy-go-lucky childlike ally who can remind them of the importance of delight and play.

This outcome is obviously different from the feared outcome— that the negative, bad, or wrong-thinking parts of ourselves must not be loved or they will take over. The only time that does happen, in fact, is when those parts have to speak louder and louder, because we are not listening to their messages. Really listening to all our parts—and especially knowing and actively loving our shortcomings—is the key to unconditional love for ourselves. Note that loving your shortcomings will not make them disappear—it will just make them feel like allies instead of enemies. How that works will be apparent when you do the Love Experiment.

Experimenting with Love

It's time to introduce a powerful experiment, one that you'll do three times this week—once for yourself, once for those in your calling circle, and once for your calling (each version is presented separately, as they are slightly different). The point of the Love Experiment for Yourself is twofold—to listen to your shortcomings and to love them—so that your love for yourself can be truly unconditional.

⚗ Love Experiment for Yourself

Goal: To explicitly record your shortcomings as of right now and love them until they feel like allies.

Time required: 30 minutes

In this experiment, you will be listening hard, recording truths, and loving with abandon. You don't have to do it 100 percent right—and you don't have to complete it. (Pro tip: No one is actually aware of all their shortcomings, so working with a few representative ones is just fine.)

1. Review your notes.

    We did a little work on assessing your shortcomings in Week 6, when you contacted members of your calling circle and took notes about your shortcomings. Take a moment to look back in your lab notebook at what you wrote down during that exercise. Circle any shortcoming that still rings true.

2. Brainstorm what's missing.

   Access your superconscious and ask for help going through your list of shortcomings. Brainstorm shortcomings that might be missing. Access trust and discernment as well. Think of anything you say, do, think, or feel that, in your opinion, is not ideal. For example, "I forget that I need breaks during the day," "I pull out my hair at night when I'm nervous," "I often fail to give others the benefit of the doubt," "I get angry when really I'm just afraid," and so on.

3. Stop your list and look at underlying shortcomings.

   When you think you've got a good group to work with, declare your list done for now (it's never really done, of course) and take a look at what you have. Then ask yourself whether there are any underlying shortcomings that might be responsible for two or more of the shortcomings on your list. For example, "No breaks and pulling out my hair are both related to not treating my body with respect." Try to get to the most basic level with your shortcomings, so you only have a few that underlie the longer list. (Hint: Almost every perceived shortcoming is caused by not loving ourselves. It's okay if you can't make that link every time—but try to see if you can.)

4. Rewrite a master list of general, underlying shortcomings.

   On a new page, write out a list of general, underlying short-comings—these are the ones you found in step 3.

5. Listen to the needs of each shortcoming on your master list.

   In your inner lab, sit down each shortcoming on your master list and ask it what it would need to feel loved. Listen intently to the answers, jotting down responses next to each shortcoming on your master list. Once you have the responses, see if you can give what is needed to each shortcoming and if you can love it actively. Just try that and see if you can. If not, that's okay. Trying actually helps a lot.

6. Love your specific shortcomings.

   Go back and look at the list you made in step 2. Explicitly try to love each one of those shortcomings too. Note in your lab notebook how that goes for you. Again, if some of them are more difficult to love than others, write about it.

7. Discover your allies.

   Looking back at the list of your master shortcomings, ask yourself: "How is this shortcoming an ally in disguise? When it arises, what is it trying to tell me?" For example, when the shortcoming of "Sometimes I don't treat my body with respect" arises in your awareness, maybe it is trying to tell you that it's time to take a nap!

8. Celebrate with all of your allies.

   Back in your inner lab, pack in with you all your allies—the general ones, the specific ones, any others that show up—and start jumping up and down. Maybe turn on some music and dance with your allies. Celebrate the love you have among you!

The Love Experiment is something you can do any time a new crop of shortcomings emerges in your life. The basic principle is to assume that every part of you has a reason to be with you, including your shortcomings. Accepting all of them into the fold and loving them will turn them into helpful allies—every time. You may still smoke cigarettes, yell at people when you're tired, and get triggered when other people don't trust you—but when these behaviors crop up, more and more you'll say to them something like, "Oh, hi, you! That's right—I remember now what you're trying to tell me. I need to take a nap."

In the following section you'll apply the same practice and logic to your calling circle—you'll learn to listen to and love the shortcomings of those in your circle and, in so doing, turn those shortcomings into allies as well.

Loving Others

This is an experiment-heavy week, so let's keep going. Once you have the hang of trying to do the Love Experiment for Yourself, you're ready to try it with your calling circle. It doesn't matter that you haven't completely acknowledged and loved every single one of your shortcomings—it's the spirit of trying and the positively euphoric feeling that agape creates that allows us to keep going.

In the Love Experiment for Others, we're going toward a similar goal—knowing and loving the shortcomings of others—but it takes slightly different steps to get there. In this experiment, you don't have to tell anyone you know and love about what you believe their shortcomings are. It'll be internal to you. But it's still very powerful.

 Love Experiment for Others

Goal: To explicitly acknowledge what you perceive as the short-comings of those in your calling circle and love those shortcomings until they feel like allies.

Time required: 30 minutes

In this experiment, you are risking creating close relationships—closer than you've had before—because any perceived shortcomings of the others in your calling circle are going to draw you closer to them rather than push you away. As you read these words, notice if you're scared. If you are, good work! You understand the power of love. It's both exciting and terrifying—and it's not owned by anyone. Get ready to access some!

1. Go into your inner lab.

    Enter your inner lab and make yourself comfortable. Mentally surround yourself with the people in your calling circle. Make sure you know where each one sits. Draw out the seating arrangements in your lab notebook so you are very clear about it.

2. Record the shortcomings.

Access trust and discernment, and begin with yourself. Next to your name in your lab notebook, write down your major short-comings—the underlying ones. Now move to the person to your left. Next to their name in your lab notebook, write down a few examples of things they do that, in your mind, represent their shortcomings. This is not a time to pretend you don't notice annoying things that other people do. If you can't think of any shortcomings, choose one for them that is the same as one of yours. You'll never have to show them this notebook or talk with them about what you wrote down. After you're done with the first person, move clockwise around the circle, doing the same for each. For example, some shortcomings common in calling circles might be, "She doesn't listen as well as I'd like," "He keeps thinking I'm like him but I'm different," "She is afraid to tell me the truth."

3. Rewrite a master list of general, underlying shortcomings.

On a new page, write out a list of general, underlying short-comings for the whole group—these are underlying the specific shortcomings of one or more persons. There could be just one—or several—underlying shortcoming for the whole group. For example, you might write, "Not listening and being afraid to tell me the truth are similar, in that I feel they are both about not respecting my need for a clear communication channel."

4. Listen to the needs.

As in the Love Experiment for Yourself, sit down each general shortcoming on your calling circle master list and ask it what it would need to feel loved. Listen intently to the answers, jotting down responses next to each shortcoming on your master list. Once you have the responses, see if you can give what is needed to each shortcoming and if you can love it actively. Again, just try—trying makes a huge difference in this experiment.

5. Love their specific shortcomings.

   Go back and look at the list you made in step 2. Explicitly try to love each one of those more specific shortcomings as well. Note how this goes for you in your lab notebook.

6. Discover your allies.

   Looking back at your master list of calling circle shortcomings, ask yourself of each one: "How is this shortcoming an ally in disguise? When it arises, what is it trying to tell me?" For example, when "They are not respecting my need for a clear communication channel" arises in your awareness, maybe this shortcoming is trying to tell you that you need to speak out loud your wish for a clear communication channel in your calling circle.

7. Call your calling circle.

   Contact those in your calling circle and in your way, let them know that you love them. No need to tell them any of the shortcomings you wrote down for them. Those are really just perceived shortcomings, not necessarily reflecting actuality. Instead, tell them how it feels to be connected to them in this circle and how it feels to love this circle unconditionally.

You might have noticed that experimenting with loving others is really another way to experiment with loving yourself. We may tell ourselves that the shortcomings of others are unrelated to our own shortcomings—they are not "our fault." And that's true, for most people. But when it comes to the people you choose to be in your calling circle, it's worth remembering that by consciously choosing them to join you as support for your calling, their shortcomings were specifically selected by you to become the perfect allies in your work. Excellent choice!

Loving Your Calling

It's no accident that we're going through these three experiments in a specific order. As suggested in the first insight, looking at and loving your shortcomings has to happen first, so you can access unconditional love and use it to love others. Once you are accessing unconditional love, knowing and loving those in your calling circle is necessary before you can risk loving your calling itself.

Why? We are primarily social creatures. Many of us have concerns that our calling is not going to be acceptable to other people. Sure, we've worked on this before, but the concern is likely to show up in many different ways. By first loving your calling circle and seeing its shortcomings as allies, you will put yourself in a position to feel safe enough to fall in deep love, or even deeper love, with your calling. The support is there, the allies have shown up—so it's safe to give your life over to this work.

Insight: Loving your calling is a risk because there's no going back.

There's really no going back once you love your calling. Once you fall in love and feel close to your calling, some part of you knows that there will be no excuses, no hedges, and no changes of mind. There's only going forward and doing it. That's why the Love Experiment for Your Calling is the last one to do—it's the one most of us fear the most.

♏ The Love Experiment for Your Calling

Goal: To explicitly acknowledge what you perceive as the shortcomings of your calling, to love those shortcomings until they feel like allies, and to use those allies to energize your calling.

Time required: 30 minutes

Here we go—you can do it! This is the moment you've been waiting for. You're holding back no longer; you're committing to your calling as your true work. This commitment is based in love, and it will supercharge your calling. If you're not afraid, go to straight to step 1, right now. And if you are afraid? Go straight to step 1, right now.

1. Go into your inner lab.

    Enter your inner lab and make yourself comfortable. In your lab notebook, write down your calling in the center of a new page.

2. Record the shortcomings.

    Access trust and discernment. Ask yourself, "In what ways is my calling not okay? What important work does my calling exclude? How might my calling fail?" Write down your answers in the space around where you wrote your calling. For instance, you might write, "My calling won't really help poor people, it is too broad, it is too focused on me, and it will never be achieved because it's too ambitious."

3. Rewrite a master list of general, underlying shortcomings.

    On a new page, write out a list of general, underlying short-comings for your calling. These compose the master list of the underlying ways that your calling falls short, in your percep-tion. Continuing with the above example, you might write, "Not being too broad and not ever being achieved are part of the same underlying shortcoming—my calling can feel too big. Also, being too focused on me and not helping poor people are part of the same shortcoming—my calling can feel selfish."

4. Listen to the needs of each shortcoming on your master list.

    Again, sit down each master-list shortcoming and ask it what it would need to feel loved. Listen intently to the answers, jotting down responses next to each shortcoming on your master list. Once all the responses are in, try to give each one what is needed while also loving it.

5. Love your calling's specific shortcomings.

   Go back and look at the list you made in step 2 and explicitly try to love each one of those more specific shortcomings as well. Write down how this works for you. Circle any specific shortcoming that you have a difficult time loving.

6. Discover your allies.

   Looking back at your master list of calling shortcomings, ask yourself of each one, "How is this shortcoming an ally in disguise? When it arises in my awareness, what is it trying to tell me?" For example, when the shortcoming "My calling feels selfish" arises in your awareness, it might be trying to remind you that you deserve love too.

7. Create with your calling.

   Go to a new page in your lab notebook and write your calling in the center. Surround your calling with the names of all your newfound allies. Draw or write about the things they can now remind you to recognize and the actions they can remind you to take.

Congratulations! You have almost completed energizing your calling. Whenever you feel your calling is stalled out, you can revisit this page in your lab notebook and see for yourself what shortcomings and allies are being activated in your awareness. By remembering to love all of the shortcomings and pay attention to the wisdom that this love reveals, your engine will be almost fully revved and ready for action!

Conclusion

Wonderful work this week! You've charged up your calling with love, and you have gained awareness of your shortcomings as well as the allies that they can become when they are loved. You have also experienced what it feels like to access unconditional love and to use that love to shift your calling into go mode.

To finalize the energizing of your calling, next week we'll close out this part of the program with work designed to clarify and amplify your natural talents. After all the work you've done with your shortcomings this week, you are probably ready for the delight that comes with exploring your unique gifts. So dig in!

WEEK 8

Your Gifts, Your Calling

Objective: To create both an inventory of your natural gifts and a handy user's guide to the inner workings of your calling.

Opening Your Gifts

You've done important and truly difficult work during the past seven weeks. This week, we'll integrate all of it. First, you'll celebrate your unique, natural talents: the gifts that come without effort. Then you'll draw on your discoveries during the past seven weeks to create a model of your calling by building a *user's guide* specific to the unique mechanics of your true work. You'll turn to this user's guide during the last four weeks of this program and beyond.

This is a brief chapter—it is all action, no pondering. At this point, you are ready to integrate what you've learned. You can set up your model of your calling so that it is ready to engage the world. Speaking of engagement with the world, for the work in the second part of this chapter, you'll need an Internet-enabled device (laptop or tablet would work best) to create the user's guide for your calling.

Defining Your Gifts

Your gifts are those skills that you draw on without trying. They are your natural talents, and they are almost always available to you. In this section, you'll work on defining your gifts.

While it can be a lot of fun, trying to list your natural talents can also be a bit mystifying. For instance, if you are the first to raise your hand at meetings to express your viewpoint, you might have the gift of being assertive, the gift of leadership, or both. Pinpointing your exact gifts is critical for the care and feeding of your calling, because you will rely on your gifts over and over again. Sticking with the car analogy, if love is your engine, your gifts are like premium fuel.

> **Insight:** Even though you use your gifts without trying, they are among the most effective tools you have.

It takes three action steps to create an inventory of your gifts. First, you'll need to comb your memory to briefly describe your *operating requirements*—the baseline needs that must be met so that you can access your natural talents. Second, you'll need the full authority of your authentic self to spot your gifts. Your gifts can be a bit difficult to see, because you're swimming in the water of your natural talents all the time, which has the effect of making them almost invisible. Third, you'll need your calling circle, including your trust and love for yourself and them, to help make sure your gift inventory is both complete and accurate. Three brief exercises can accomplish these steps. Try to do them all on the same day.

Brief Exercise

Let's get clear about your operating requirements. This is a quick exercise based on years of experience being yourself.

1.   Get your lab notebook and a pen.

2. Quickly jot down two to ten conditions that you require for you to function as yourself on a given day. For example, nine hours of sleep, hydration, food every five hours, thirty minutes of cardio, at least an hour puttering.

3. Once you have your list, read it out loud. Cross out anything that is not a requirement—and underscore everything that is truly necessary.

4. Title this list "Operating Requirements" and go directly on to the next exercise.

If you need to take care of one of your operating requirements right now, do that and come right back. If not, keep going to the next exercise.

Brief Exercise

It's time to open your gifts! You'll use the full authority of your authentic self to brainstorm a list of your natural talents.

1. Turn to a new page in your lab notebook and get ready to write or draw.

2. Go into your inner lab and look around. Gather all of your authentic self, so you feel your energy and your authority focused right where you are, in your inner lab. Where would you most like to be in your inner lab during this exercise? Go to your favorite spot, but don't sit down. You'll be moving around in this exercise.

3. Tell your superconscious that you're making a list of your gifts—the natural talents that are like second nature to you. Then ask your superconscious to play a game with you.

4. The game is "gift charades." Here's how it works. Your conscious mind and your superconscious are actors on a stage,

acting out each of the gifts embedded in your authentic self. Either you or your superconscious can start the action, and the other one will join in until you both agree that you've got the gift described correctly. (Note for people who aren't visual thinkers: the game can be "gift discussion" or "gift songwriting" instead of "gift charades," if you like. The crucial point is to play the game with your superconscious and make sure you agree on the description of your gift.) For example, you might be thinking, "Let me see, what is my superconscious doing? Pouring water for me? Ah! I get it. I have the gift of hospitality—I like people to have what they want and to feel comfortable. I'll try giving some love to my superconscious to see how that goes. No, wait, my superconscious is now showing me a more subtle element of this gift—when I offer the love to my superconscious, it glows, it's all healthy. I get it now! It's saying that I have the gift of healing. I love to heal people, and I'm good at it—with words, nourishment, and love. My superconscious is cheering for me now—okay, that means we agree. I'll write down 'healing with words, nourishment, and love' in my lab notebook. Onto the next!"

5. Keep playing until you have an inventory of at least five gifts and you've had a blast.

Your inventory is probably close to accurate, but it's also important to get some wisdom from your calling circle. If you're like most people, your supporters will be more aware of your gifts than you are. So now you'll do a brief exercise to find out whether your gift inventory is accurate, according to those who know you well and support your calling.

Brief Exercise

Let's check these gifts out. It's time to contact at least two members of your calling circle and ask them to answer some brief questions.

1. Choose a member of your calling circle to contact; keep your gift inventory handy.

2. Contact that person and tell them you are checking out whether you have completed an accurate inventory of your natural talents. Explain that these are ways of being or things you do that come naturally to you and are accessible to you most of the time. Then tell them your list of gifts and any notes you have about them. Finally, ask them to answer these questions:

   • Are any gifts missing? If so, what are they?

   • Do any of these gifts seem like subsets of a larger, more encompassing gift?

   • Do any of these gifts seem like they are actually distinct gifts that should be broken out separately?

   • Do any of these gifts seem to not come naturally to me?

   • Do any of these gifts seem inaccurately defined?

3. Write down their answers.

4. Go back to step 1 until you have contacted and received responses from at least two people in your calling circle.

5. Take your notes from those in your calling circle and go into your inner lab. Recall your love and trust for them. Also recall your love and trust for yourself. Using your trust and love of yourself as well as your discernment, edit your gift inventory. Now read your inventory out loud, listening for truth and checking for your truth reaction. If you feel it, that's perfect. You're done. If not, keep editing and reading aloud until you feel your truth reaction.

Now that you have completed your vetted gift inventory, you're ready to create your user's guide. You may feel mystified as to how you will build this guide, but, after all the work you've done, you actually know more about the unique mechanics of your calling than you have ever known before. Still, you don't know everything yet. There's a lot to learn, as always. But there's also a lot you have already learned—and you're about to discover the practical benefit of your gathered wisdom.

Creating Your User's Guide

Because your calling is a process, it has dynamics; it changes over time and reacts to outside forces in predictable and sometimes unpredictable ways. Some of those responses will feel right on track, others will feel uncomfortable or wrong. Your user's guide is what you will turn to when things don't feel like they're working well. Your user's guide is based on what you've already learned about how certain events are likely to help or hinder your progress as you pursue your calling.

You can't predict everything that will happen as you engage your calling in the world. But you can make some educated guesses based on what you know about yourself and the tools you've used so far, and as you create your user's guide you'll draw upon these guesses. Your user's guide will let you get back on your path and in the flow, even when you inevitably swerve to the side or feel stuck.

♟ User's Guide

Goal: To create a unique and helpful guide for the operation of your calling.

Time required: 1 to 2 hours

Recommended: Internet-enabled device (ideally not a smartphone)

This experiment is a truly integrative step. If you balk at the time commitment, trust that it is well worth it. When you're done, you'll have a personalized manual to help you move forward on your true path in the days, weeks, and years ahead. Your user's guide won't be perfect, and it will need updating from time to time, but that's to be expected. Even if you were to never look at it again, creating it does the same work as model building does for scientists—it gives you the satisfaction that you have really understood a process, in this case how your calling works. Get ready to reveal to yourself the deep discoveries you have already made about your calling.

1. Go to http://www.thecallingprogram.com.

   Click on "User's Guide to Your Calling." Follow the instructions on the screen, which are also given below. If you choose to complete these steps offline, please use clean sheets of paper that you can bind together into a guide when you are done.

2. Get your lab notebook and go into your inner lab.

   You'll need your lab notebook, so you have access to all your notes from the past seven weeks. Enter your inner lab and make yourself comfortable. Try to be in the full authority of your authentic self. Be sure to access trust, love, and discernment while you sift through your notes and complete the following steps.

3. Record what you have learned.

   Record your calling, your currently active calling circle members, your deal-makers and deal-breakers, your major shortcomings and their related allies, your operating requirements, and your gifts—all copied directly from your lab notebook. As you copy these words, notice if anything feels off or needs changing. If so, sit with your changes, say them out loud, and feel if you have your truth reaction. Once you do, make the change and move on.

4. Anticipate the path of your calling.

   This step puts you in prediction mode. While you can't necessarily predict how external forces will influence the progress of your calling, you can predict how you are likely to react to any arrows of misfortune or feathers of fortune. Make sure you are centered in your authentic self and claiming your own authority—still in your inner lab—as you answer these fill-in-the-blank questions:

When I _____, the tool that works best to get me back on my path is _____. The most clarifying insight for me at these times is _____. My fear about taking action to shift my experience is _____, with the mirror fear of _____. My helpful gifts during this time are _____, and my most useful calling circle supports in this situation are _____. What needs more love and trust is probably _____. And what is within my authority to change is _____. With all of myself, I pledge that, in this situation, I choose to _____.

Although you can include additional situations, the recommended minimum situations to include in your user's guide are:

   a. When I feel uncomfortable feelings
   b. When I don't feel anything
   c. When I don't know my next action
   d. When I feel arrogant
   e. When I feel disconnected from my calling
   f. When I feel overwhelmed by my calling

As you contemplate each situation, imagine yourself having that experience a year in the future. Ask yourself what tools you will use to help move yourself forward, and fill in the blanks with the tools that you tell yourself are most important. You can use any of the tools explored in this program or others that you've learned elsewhere. The idea is to select ones that are likely to work for you in each situation. On the website, all the tools and insights provided in this book are listed for you to choose from, as well as areas to write in your own. Be honest. Choose tools that you think work best—it can be the same tool every time, or you can use new tools for each situation. Remember that this user's guide is meant to provide both a model of the mechanics of your calling as well as a place to go in the future to troubleshoot—so be as honest as you can be with yourself, while avoiding the tendency to try to get it exactly right. Few people follow their user's guide to the letter when troubleshooting a process—but it's handy to have around because it does teach you something every so often.

Here is an example: When I feel lonely, the tool that works best to get me back on my path is to go into my inner lab and talk with myself. The most clarifying insight for me at these times is that a useful way to manage any uncomfortable feeling is to first feel it fully, then observe it, record it, and get curious about it. My fear about taking action to shift my experience is that this won't work—I will always feel lonely, with the mirror fear of if I become un-lonely I will have to be with myself and other people. My helpful gifts during this time are doing art and enjoying music with other people, and my most useful calling circle supports in this situation are calling Joan and taking a weekly class with other people. What needs more love and trust is probably the child part of myself, who feels alone a lot. And what is within my authority to change is how much time I spend shaming and judging the lonely part of myself. With my whole self, I pledge that, in this situation, I choose to actively love the child part of myself and give it a gift every day, and to do something regularly that requires me to be with other people.

5. Check your work.

   Go over everything you've written and be sure it represents your current understanding by reading it aloud. As you do, check whether you get your truth reaction much of the time. If so, you're set. If not, work with your superconscious to change whatever it is that needs changing.

6. Print out your guide and write down how you feel.

   Once done, print out your user's guide. Write down in your lab notebook how it felt to create your user's guide and what your thoughts are about using it in the future.

Your user's guide is unique. Because it's personalized for you, no one can tell you exactly how to use it. Maybe you'll never look at it again. Or perhaps you'll experiment with cracking it open once or twice when you're frustrated by something during the next few weeks. Maybe you'll decorate it with art, bind it together as a book, print out copies for your friends and family, and each day read it as a reminder of your calling. There's no right way to use it—but creating it at all is a victory, because you've really integrated everything you've learned so far.

Conclusion

In these eight weeks of the program, you've claimed your calling, energized it, and created a manual for its operation in the world. What more could you need? Continuing the scientist analogy, you've been working on your postdoctoral training in this portion of the Calling program. Now you still need to get to the main event: independently launching your work into the world.

The final portion of this program gets you to the point where you are actively engaging your calling and letting it do its work. It's a journey that will require everything you've learned so far and more—so it's fortunate you've now got that wisdom encapsulated in your user's guide.

PART III

Engage Your Calling

Finally! It's time to launch your calling, independently, out in the world. This is the moment you've been moving toward all along. What else do you need to learn?

All this time you've been working on your understanding of your calling and of yourself—your shortcomings, your gifts, and how you work in relationships with others. But engaging your calling in the world requires not just you, your calling circle, and your calling. It requires the rest of the universe to play along. Even if you build the most glorious user's guide, with all the bells and whistles, if the rest of the universe doesn't play along, your calling will not be productively engaged. It will be like building a car without ever driving it.

Your true work is a process, and, as any process works, it transforms the universe. These final four weeks are about fine-tuning your relationship with the universe, connecting your calling in time and space, and learning to surrender to the rest of the universe to get the hardest work of your calling done. At the end, you'll celebrate your fully engaged calling.

Preparing Your Relationship with the Universe

Objective: To create a playful, positive, and productive relationship with the rest of the universe.

What Is the Universe?

It's time to turn your attention toward the universe outside you and your calling circle. It's not that you don't need to maintain your relationships with yourself and your close supporters—you do and you will—but you can't really engage your calling unless it's working out there, in the universe. So far you have the rules that support your calling, plus lots more skills than you had at the beginning of this program. Your calling has been fully energized but not yet engaged.

So why the shift from "world" to "universe"? The word "universe" works better than "world" to describe everything, because with the Internet we have become so global in our thinking that "world" sounds accessible and small. "Universe" sounds appropriately large and inclusive. Of course, you and everyone you know are contained within the universe; but here, when thinking about your relationship with the universe, it's useful to separate the part we've worked on so far—you and your calling circle—from the environment in which you and your calling circle find yourselves.

It's kind of like developing a relationship with your supercon-scious—even though it is part of you, you relate to it differently than other parts of you. In this case, you are part of the universe but you relate to the universe differently than how you relate to other groups you are part of or other projects you participate in.

What is the universe like? Well, it includes everything that exists: thoughts, feelings, objects, electromagnetic fields, particles, waves, frogs, clouds, people, meteors, space junk, ocean junk, neg-ative ideas and actions, positive ideas and actions, black holes, and so on. But what is it, essentially? In this program the universe is defined as having three critical features: inclusivity, connectiv-ity, and autonomy.

> **Insight:** The universe includes you and everything else. It can be in relationship to you and everything else, and its behavior is not predictable from its parts— no part of it has complete control over its actions.

The "universe" can also be used as a code name for "God." Thinking of the universe and God as the same thing can work if you define God as everything that exists, as an entity capable of connecting with you and everyone else, and as operating beyond your control. If this sounds like your definition of God, when you read "universe" in this book, it might be useful for you to think "God." You also might not have this definition of God. If you don't, and if you don't believe in God, in this section of the program you can just read "universe" as it has already been described.

But what if you believe in God, but you don't believe God is the same as the universe? Well, that can work too. If the universe contains everything that exists, God would be part of the uni-verse. Within the universe, God could be a superset or a subset. If God were a superset, God would contain everything else in the universe but still be part of the universe—God would be like a "wrapper" for the universe. If God were a subset, God would be contained within the rest of the universe. Regardless, God would be part of the universe, because here we're defining the universe as everything that exists.

Even if you don't believe in God, the God conversation may make you wonder who is in control of this universe, as it is defined here. Research on complex adaptive systems tells us that the behaviors of the individual parts of the system can be unpredictable and powerfully shift the behavior of the entire system (Holden 2005). So when the question "Who controls this entire complex adaptive system of the universe?" is asked, it can only be answered with "The system itself is the controller." If you think that God exists as part of the universe, then God would exert control through being either a superset or subset of the system. So regardless of how God relates to the given definition of "universe" for you, you'll need to work on your relationship with the universe in order to engage your calling in a productive way. Let's get to that!

Assessing Your Relationship with the Universe

Wait—if the universe includes frogs and rocks and electromagnetism, why is it necessary to have a good relationship with the entire universe? Your calling only relates to a small subset of what's in the universe, after all. Having a good relationship with the entire thing seems like a lot of unnecessary work.

There are two important insights this question surfaces. First, the question shows that it's easy to think of the universe outside ourselves and our close friends and family as a "thing" or an object, but it's not. It contains lots of people and other animals that have their own subjective experiences. Thinking of other beings as objects will not get you far in your calling, because one key to engaging your calling is to open up to avenues presented to you from the inner spaces contained in the folks around you. Second, even if you don't think of animals and people as objects, the universe contains actual objects that you probably already have a relationship with: your technological devices, your bed, your home, and your clothes, to name a few that most people have.

Let's take technology as an example. Anecdotally, every scientist, engineer, and technologist knows that having a positive relationship with your technology will make things run much more smoothly for you. Countless are the times when people take their devices to specialists who can find no problem with them, even though the problem was clearly manifest minutes before, in the hands of their owners. The difference? Maybe it's coincidence, but this effect is so consistent that it seems as if the specialist just has a different relationship to technology than the owner. It's as if there's something real about the relationship we have with technology. And this idea can apply to every element of the universe. Regardless of whether this is a false feeling or not, we do know that positive relationships with anyone and anything are better for us than negative ones, and they are *way* more fun.

> **Insight:** Pursuing positive relationships with everything in the universe is not only effective for engaging your calling—it's fun!

Trying to create positive relationships with all the people, things, ideas, and feelings in the universe is both productive and fun. It's fun because you will learn a lot about yourself and others, and you will be forced to laugh a lot. It's productive because your efforts will pay off in actually producing positive relationships. These positive relationships will assist the growth of your true work, creating the changes in the universe that your calling is specifically designed to create.

Damien: Positivizing the Crap out of Life

Damien is a gifted philosopher of technology who is pursuing his PhD in a multidisciplinary graduate program. When I interviewed him at an immersive workshop we were both attending, he was passionate about understanding how cultural shifts are being made by technologies such as robotics and artificial intelligence, as well as how cultural biases are influencing which technologies are made and how technology is used.

When I asked him to put his calling into words, he said, "It's to bridge worlds and generate understanding." As you'll see from his story, he's done exactly that, and he's done it by working toward a positive relationship with the universe while using understanding as his key principle.

Damien recalled that even in third grade, "I felt compelled to make people understand why 'acting out' behavior in a classmate was not something to be punished but something to be understood as the only way that person could get a need met." He described how he once intervened physically to protect another child from a bully, and he had had a hard time explaining to his parents why this had to be done.

In high school, Damien had a bad experience. He was new in a city, at a new school, and didn't like anyone. He had negative relationships, and the feelings were mutual. He didn't try to create positive relationships because he reasoned that doing so was pointless while in a negative environment. His fix was to leave that place to give him some distance and to find positive relationships. On reflection, Damien said that if he hadn't done that, the teachers who meant so much to him at his second high school would never have come into his life. "At my second high school, my desire to understand evolved into a desire to teach—because I could see that teaching was all about understanding the audience well enough to get them to understand what is being taught. As a teacher now, I find myself trying to find those places where there's miscommunication and working toward helping students recognize the misunderstanding to help protect their progress toward learning."

When I asked him whether he's ever lost the thread of his purpose or felt that perhaps people don't have reasons for *their behavior, he told me, "There are plenty of times when I had to pull myself back from a knee-jerk reaction because I was angry or insulted. But I know that just reacting without understanding won't solve anything. There is so much of an external push to Balkanize—to create us-versus-them scenarios—that what I have to do to get back on track is to remind myself that we'll all be better off if we understand. Even those who have been in power dominance for a while need to be understood." Damien has good insight into power dominance dynamics, as he is a black man living in the US. "Sometimes I want to throw up my hands or I go into despair. Sometimes what works is I have to wallow a bit—go sit with my despair, be angry and upset. As I move through those feelings, I can clarify the facts of the situation. And then I go on."*

I asked Damien what he'd tell his third-grade self, if he had the chance to talk with himself, knowing what he knows about his calling now. "Everybody understands things at different times. Just because they understand this one thing that you see as connected, it doesn't mean they'll understand other things. Understanding comes in pieces, and it takes time."

Damien's story shows that creating a positive relationship with the universe does not mean letting people violate your deal-breakers. It does not mean tolerating negative actions in your environment or even challenging yourself to remain somewhere that triggers you to act out. What it does mean is that you challenge yourself to move to a place where you can have a positive relationship with everything in the universe. That could mean you do what Damien did when he switched to another high school—you physically take yourself somewhere that will work better for creating positive relationships, and you understand your previously negative relationships, given the new distance. It could also mean that you stay in a relationship with someone who acts negatively by appreciating how their actions teach you about your own boundaries. In other words, being in a positive relationship with the rest of the universe does not mean you pretend that things that are not good are somehow good. It means challenging yourself to create good out of the things that already exist.

Insight: A positive relationship with the rest of the universe relies on making a commitment to find the good in what exists, right now.

Taking inspiration from Damien's impressive ability to understand and transform his experience, let's do an exercise meant to bring out any rough spots in your relationship with the universe and move you toward making your relationship more positive.

Brief Exercise

Let's identify your rough spots in your relationship with the universe.

1. Get your lab notebook and go into your inner lab.

2. Find an insightful place in your inner lab—you're about to get some good insights and you want to be ready to experiment with them. For example, if your inner lab is a garden, you might go to the fountain where information can emerge. If your inner lab is a laboratory, go to the lab bench.

3. Once in your insightful place, look, listen, and sense any insights that arise in answer to the question: What bothers me about the way the universe is right now? You might see an image or hear song lyrics or sense foreboding—write down in your lab notebook everything, without editing. Keep doing this until nothing else comes up.

4. Now look at your list of insights and form them into an answer or answers to the original question. What are these insights trying to tell you about your relationship to the universe? For example, as insights, you may have written: "a scared feeling," "Oh no!" "someone drowning." You then ask yourself, "What

are these insights trying to tell me about my complaints about my relationship with the universe?" After a few moments the answer comes: "I'm scared that the universe outside of me is so big it will swallow me up."

5. Read your answer or answers to the question about your relationship to the universe. Do you have your truth reaction? If so, you're done with the exercise. If not, keep listening for the answer and testing out potential answers until you get your truth reaction.

Getting to the essential nature of any complaint you currently have about the rest of the universe is necessary for our next step, which is to address this complaint and begin to enter into a positive, playful, and productive relationship with the rest of the universe.

Shifting Your Relationship with the Rest of the Universe

It bears repeating that shifting your relationship with the rest of the universe does not require you to falsely claim that you enjoy being around everything and everyone in the universe or pretending not to have boundaries. Nor does it require that you have only feelings that are "positive." In fact, it requires that you use all of the skills and tools that you've learned so far, including continuing to be aware of your deal-makers and deal-breakers in relationships, and experiencing, accepting, and loving all of your feelings. But it also requires something else—a strong commitment to a new habit.

The commitment required to improve your relationship with the universe asks that you adopt the Positivity Habit. This habit has five easy-to-learn steps:

1. Observe, experience, and accept your feelings so that you can notice when you are in a negative relationship with any person, animal, object, action, idea, or feeling.

2. When you notice a negative relationship, ask yourself to accept that this person, animal, object, action, idea, or feeling exists in the universe right now.

3. Determine whether you will remain near or around this person, animal, object, action, idea, or feeling right now. You may not have a choice in your location or your relationships, so determine whether you will remain near this element of the universe, rather than asking yourself what you want.

4. Regardless of whether you do remain near this element of the universe, appreciate what this person, animal, object, action, idea, or feeling can teach you. Appreciate the positive feeling born out of knowing that you are learning from this element of the universe.

5. Allow that positive feeling to infuse your relationship with this person, animal, object, action, idea, or feeling.

These five steps may seem like a fair amount to do if you have a lot of negative relationships with elements of the universe. But once you do the Positivity Habit a few times, it becomes second nature and won't feel like an effort at all. To see whether a commitment to the Positivity Habit works for you, try the Commitment Experiment.

⚗ Commitment Experiment

Goal: To discover how making the commitment to be in a positive relationship with the universe works for you.

Time required: 5–15 minutes

Welcome to the rest of your life! It may sound dramatic, but this experiment will get you going on shifting your relationship with the rest of the universe. And if you keep this habit of positivity and the commitment to pursue it, you will be ready for wild success in engaging your calling.

1. Go into your inner lab and make it wonderful in there.

    Surrounding yourself with beautiful and nourishing images and sounds in your inner lab will help sustain you as you contemplate your complaint about the universe at large.

2. Get your lab notebook and read your complaint about the universe.

    Read your complaint out loud—the answer to the question about your current relationship with the universe arrived at in the brief exercise you completed earlier in this chapter.

3. Commit this one time to doing the Positivity Habit with your complaint.

    You've already done step 1—you've accepted and observed your complaint. Now accept that your complaint exists in the universe, right now. Then determine whether the complaint will remain in your vicinity. There's no right answer! Just notice what's true. Regardless of the answer, appreciate the wisdom that your complaint is teaching you. Allow the good feelings from that learning and your appreciation to infuse into your relationship with your complaint.

    For example, if your complaint is that you are afraid the universe is so big that it will swallow you up, first you admit that this complaint exists in the universe, right now. No two ways about it—there it is. Then you take a look at the complaint from all sides. "Is it headed away from me? Am I headed away from it? Or are we sticking together?" You notice that you're sticking together—practically holding hands! Okay, it looks like you'll remain in its vicinity.

    Next, you ask the complaint what it can teach you. After a bit of silence, it tells you that it is teaching you about humility and also about your own power. The meaning of this is not totally clear to you, but that's okay—you can understand that it is teaching you something, and you can appreciate it for that. Finally, you let the positive feeling about this learning connection fill you up; you put that feeling in your relationship, in between you and the complaint. You hold hands a bit and it feels good.

4. Write down how it felt and make a commitment.

In your lab notebook, record how it felt to commit to the Positivity Habit this one time. If it felt good, make a commitment to trying the Positivity Habit two more times this week and recording the results. If it didn't feel good, ask yourself to redo step 3, but this time with your experience of this experiment as your complaint. Then come back to this step. If it still didn't feel good, brainstorm what you will do instead of the Positivity Habit to pursue a positive relationship with the rest of the universe; commit to trying out one of your ideas three times this week and recording the results.

You'll use this transformative habit—either the Positivity Habit or the one you've invented for yourself—for the rest of your life and certainly for the rest of this program.

With the Positivity Habit, you are making a commitment to positively shift a negative relationship with any element in the universe at least three times this week. It's worth noting that such shifts take place in the present moment. The effects of these shifts don't always extend to the future, so do not be surprised if you end up shifting the same relationship more than once. That's to be expected. Over time, you'll find these present-moment shifts will evolve into lasting shifts. Often the relationships that will most support your calling end up being the ones that took you a repeated effort to shift. You can look forward to discovering how positive connections with these people, animals, objects, actions, ideas, and feelings will propel the work of your calling in the universe.

Conclusion

It feels delightful to recognize that what exists is really there and that you can learn from everything. It's freeing—you no longer need to fear the reality that you cannot control the universe. You can just acknowledge your lack of control and the existence of uncomfortable people, animals, objects, actions, ideas, and feelings, and actually turn their existence into a positive experience: learning something new.

Now that you're beginning to get in the habit of creating this richly positive environment for your calling, you're ready for the nuts and bolts of engaging your calling in the universe. Next week, you'll engage your calling by creating connections in time and space—connections that hook up the actual work of your calling with the rest of the universe.

Experimenting with Connection

Objective: To connect your calling in time and space so that your calling can do its work.

Two Types of Connections

Imagine a solar panel. Let's make it a highly efficient solar panel. It is better than any other solar panel in the universe at what it does. It can power a space station all by itself. This panel is just perfect—except its access to the sun is blocked; it's stuck on a rock on the dark side of the moon.

To use it, first we need to free it from that rock, so it can access the sun. Let's assume we can do that. Now the panel has the appropriate input. "But what use is this space junk," you might ask, "since it's not hooked up to anything on the output side?" Excellent point, you. Let's imagine it's hooked up to a green leather couch. Wires from the solar panel go into the armrest. Now are you happy? "Nope," you reply. "The armrest can't do anything with the energy!" Well, that's true. The solar panel is hooked up to something inappropriate on the output side. So we'll hook it up to a battery—but this is a special kind of battery that only exists on a millisecond time scale. It goes out of existence in a millisecond from now. You say, "Ridiculous. Still useless! You need a battery that lasts over time!" Yes! Again, great point. We'll hook it up to a battery that can charge over many days.

What have we figured out in this thought experiment? Appropriate inputs and outputs are necessary for the solar panel. As long as the solar panel is connected appropriately in time and in space, it will be very useful. Your true work is exactly the same as that solar panel.

> **Insight:** Even the most impressive calling is useless without being connected to the appropriate inputs and outputs in time and space.

Remember that your calling is a process. For this process to work, your calling must be connected across time and space to the appropriate inputs and outputs. It needs the raw materials that help it do its work (inputs), and your calling needs to produce something in the universe (outputs). What does this mean for callings that are not solar panels? Let's take a more earth-bound example.

Rachel and Galen: Connected Callings

Rachel* is a woman in her sixties, Galen* is her son and in his thirties. Rachel's calling is to be what she calls a "protector of the path"—to protect people's paths against their own doubt, social pressures, or anything that could get in the way of their progress. In this calling, as a minister, writer, teacher, and performer, she has reached people around the world with her brilliant insights. Her inputs are the wisdom traditions of the world, including her own mystical revelations. Her outputs are her writings, rituals, courses, and songs. Her outputs go out into the world directly as well as indirectly, through her son.

Galen's calling is to present to the world his mother's wisdom as well as the insights of other mystics and visionaries in a way that can make their messages broadly accessed and understood. His outputs are stories, documentaries, and interviews. Rachel's output is one of Galen's major inputs.

Nothing makes this clearer than a dream Rachel had in her mid-twenties, when she was still childless. In the dream, she was an old woman defeated by life and selling her body. There was a window she could look through that showed her a park with a streetlamp in it. Every night, she saw ruffians throw rocks at the lamp and break it, and every night she saw her teenage son set up a ladder, climb it, and put a new bulb in so it could shine. It felt like a sustainable process. When Rachel awoke, she felt that she was both the old woman and the young man—both despairing in the dark and creating the light. This interpretation was certainly correct—Rachel passionately champions the dark and also brings shining light to herself and others. But now that she actually has a son and has learned that his calling was intertwined with hers, the more literal interpretation of Rachel's dream seemed obvious.

Galen said, "My mother reads books at four times the speed I do, and she is so smart that her words often go over the heads of others. My job is to take the insights that she and others have and make them tangible for regular people." He literally allows his mother's light to shine in time and space. Rachel's connection to Galen is a connection across time—it's intergenerational and, as she noted in her dream, sustainable. And although they live part of the year in different locations and part of the year in the same town, Rachel and Galen's callings work together across space.

That's how it works for Rachel and Galen, but the inputs and outputs for your calling in time and space are unique to you. Let's find out what those inputs and outputs are for you, so you are ready to hook them up!

Brief Exercise

This activity is about figuring out appropriate inputs and outputs for your calling.

1. Get your user's guide and your lab notebook. Remind yourself of your calling, your shortcomings, and your gifts.

2. Draw a diagram in your lab notebook. Write "Calling" inside a box in the center of the page. To one side, write "Inputs" in a second box; on the other side, write "Outputs" in a third box. Remind yourself that the inputs are the raw materials your calling needs to do its work, and the outputs are the products of your calling.

3. Go into your inner lab and make the intention to discover appropriate inputs for your calling. Once you've made the intention, walk to each corner of your inner lab and pick up whatever object you find in each corner. Write these objects down under "inputs"; don't worry if they don't make sense.

4. Now make the intention to discover appropriate outputs for your calling. Then go to the center of your inner lab and notice a new object that you see in the center of your lab. Walk around it to see if it has several parts. Write down your description under "outputs." Again, don't worry if what you see doesn't make sense.

5. On a new page in your lab notebook, draw the same setup: your calling in the center, inputs and outputs on the sides. This time, use your intuition to translate the list of inputs and your description of your outputs into actual real-world inputs and outputs. For example, let's say your calling is to make people laugh. If you found a rock, a plant, a rainbow, and a horse in the four corners of your lab, and you associate all of these things with the natural world, you would write "the natural world" as one important input to your calling. But perhaps you also associate

these things with beauty, so you would write "beauty" as another input to your calling. Finally, you associate rainbows with money, so you add "money" as the final input to your calling.

Moving on to outputs, let's say you found, right in the center of your lab, a tree with three different fruits. The fruits were a tiny drum, a panda bear, and a newspaper. You associate drums with music, panda bears with loving relationships, and newspapers with writing. You list your outputs as music, loving relationships, and writing.

6. Read aloud your inputs and outputs, checking for your truth reaction. Don't forget the inputs we often assume we have, such as time, health, creativity, and emotional intelligence. If you don't get a truth reaction, go back to step 2 until you do.

7. Once you've found your candidate inputs and outputs, contact two members of your calling circle to run your inputs and outputs by them and ask if they agree; also ask if you've left anything out. Listen to their advice, see if it rings true for you, and, if so, adjust your inputs and outputs accordingly.

It should now be clear what raw materials you need for your calling and what kind of outputs your calling will produce, at least for now. These can change—a solar panel's battery can fill up and new types of improved storage devices can be invented—but for now, these are your inputs and outputs. What remains is to hook them up in space and time.

Connecting Your Calling in Space

It's easy to make sure a solar panel has access to light and is hooked up to a battery. But how do you hook up your own inputs and outputs? Just knowing what they are isn't enough. But it's not clear to most of us what would be enough, and you might be wondering if your inputs and outputs are already connected.

Let's figure out what it means to hook up your inputs and outputs, and what that feels like. When your inputs and outputs are connected to your calling and your calling is connected in time, that means you have your appropriate inputs and outputs and that these connections are sustainable over time. It feels like being in a flow state (Csikszentmihalyi 1993). If you want to be technical about it, it's a state that can be described as a generic learning engine (Kaplan and Oudeyer 2004). You feel the internally generated reward of your calling being properly engaged; your work feels effortless and joyful; you learn and then incorporate what you've learned easily. This flow experience motivates you to engage your calling during more of your waking hours.

> **Insight:** Connecting your calling in space and time allows you to enjoy a flow state when your calling is engaged, and this drives you to engage your calling more often.

If you have felt that you have been in a flow state for most of your waking hours in the past week, it's likely due to your calling being currently properly connected in space and time; you can move on to the final section this week, about working your calling. If you haven't felt that way, you'll need to hook up your inputs and outputs using practical actions as well as intentions.

Brief Exercise

Let's connect your calling in space with your inputs and outputs.

1. Get your lab notebook.

2. Go into your inner lab. Imagine all of your inputs on one side of you and all of your outputs on the other. Look at your diagram in your lab notebook for inspiration.

3. In your inner lab, imagine connecting each input, with any kind of attachment, to yourself. Here, you are the stand-in for your

calling. Take a mental note of any inputs that seem difficult to connect.

4. Now imagine connecting each output, with any kind of attachment, to yourself. Take a mental note of any outputs that seem difficult to connect.

5. Sense how it feels to be connected as a unit. Try loving the entire assembly—your inputs, your calling, and your outputs.

6. Write down any resistance to loving the assembly that came up, any difficulties connecting specific inputs or outputs, and any other notes you have about your experience in your inner lab.

7. Allow yourself to move on to action—regardless of how attaching the inputs and outputs and how loving the assembly went for you. Write down in your lab notebook one small action you will take in the next day to connect any of the inputs or outputs that are not strongly connected to your calling. These small actions are miniature experiments to get your calling used to being connected more strongly to these specific inputs and outputs.

     For example, continuing with the previous example, let's say your inputs are the natural world, beauty, and money; your outputs are music, loving relationships, and writing. You feel as if the natural world and beauty are already connected to your calling as inputs, but money is not. You write down the commitment that in the next twenty-four hours you will ask for a raise or apply for a job, so you will be better acquainted with money as an input. Meanwhile, all outputs are connected strongly except writing. So you write down that in the next twenty-four hours you'll write one paragraph of at least five sentences of the novel you keep thinking about.

8. Do each of your commitments in the next twenty-four hours and, if they feel good, make similar commitments in the following twenty-four hours.

Continuing to use your connections—drawing on your inputs for raw materials and creating your outputs—will keep your calling connected and in a flow state. However, you can't always be functioning, and you don't want your connections to die just because you need to meditate, sleep, or go on vacation! Luckily, you actually aren't a machine, although machines can make nice analogies. As perceiving humans with subjective experience and imaginations, we can create lasting connections by shifting our sense of ourselves and our callings. This shift is what I call "connecting your calling in time."

Connecting Your Calling in Time

There's nothing sustainable about trying to constantly be aware of your soul's work and the need to stay connected to appropriate inputs and outputs. To go with the solar panel analogy, you can't really be in a flow state and feel effortless if you have to constantly replace batteries.

What is needed is a way to create a sustainable method of connecting to your inputs and outputs, including a way to automatically find new and improved, more-appropriate inputs and outputs as your calling becomes more and more engaged in the universe. The only way I know to do this is to create a perspective shift that allows you to conceive of yourself and your calling as a single organism that lives in time—a being who simultaneously exists in the present, past, and future. This is like an elaboration of your single, unitary path.

Most of us imagine ourselves as our bodies and minds, maybe our souls. When someone asks us to point to ourselves, we point to our hearts, bellies, or heads. Yet, those are only the parts of us that are visually obvious right now. But consider that in many ways you were the same person two minutes ago and will be two minutes from now; three years ago and three years from now.

In fact, if you imagine a line that traces every location you've been, from your birth to the present moment, and everywhere you'll go until you die, this is what physicists would call your "world line"—your every location for the lifetime of your physical existence. Even though we point to our current bodies when asked, probably because it's the part of us that can be seen right now, it seems that most of us actually feel we are our world lines. We talk about "When I get older, I want to..." and "When I was a kid, I wanted to..." Our past and future selves are real to us, and our memories and imaginations of them influence our present.

Given this experience, for most of us it would be accurate to point to our entire world line—our past, present, and future selves—as our true selves. Once we start to experience ourselves as a combination of all three—past, present, and future—we can actually pass information among all of these aspects of ourselves. Doing this same thing with your calling allows your calling to be connected to itself in time, and it also provides the information you need at each appropriate moment so you can continue to be in flow as you work your calling.

This can be conceptually difficult to understand, so let's look at an example from my life. When I was in graduate school, one of my mentors had gone into medicine in the 1960s in the United States; she was often the only woman in many of her classes. She told me that she was at a disadvantage in her career until she figured out that there was an unspoken expectation about who researchers were and how their life paths were anticipated to go. The expectation was that all of them were men. Thus, the expected life path of researchers was: do your training in your twenties, cut your teeth in your thirties, make a niche for yourself in your forties, do service and receive awards in your fifties, and retire in your sixties.

Because she wasn't a man, my mentor was already on a different trajectory and feeling at a huge disadvantage. But then she realized that she needed to forecast her own life path, one that put her whole self—past, present, and future—in the picture. She had to create her own story, one that accounted for the children she would be raising. She would finish her training in her twenties, keep one eye out for interesting research while cutting her teeth and raising kids in her thirties, continue cutting her teeth and making a niche in her forties, make a name for herself and complete her niche in her fifties, do service and receive awards in her sixties, and, because women on average live and remain productive longer than men, retire in her seventies. Once she realized she could look at her struggles in the present and allow the future to compensate for them, she could move back into flow.

That example is specifically about using connections across time to compensate for struggle in the present, but the same is true with information. You can actually shift perspective into your future self and ask your future self what you need for your calling. Ideally, this can become an everyday habit—in fact, it's a habit of many of the successful people I have interviewed. Although my interviewees may have called the practice "visioning" or "projecting" or "prospecting," the process is the same: allowing your projection or vision of the needs and successes of your future to inform what would be useful now.

This is the only perspective shift I know, aside from next week's work with surrender, that allows your true work to be sustainably engaged in the world. So regardless of whether it sounds reasonable, please suspend disbelief and try this next brief exercise to hook up your calling with your future and past selves, in time.

Brief Exercise

Now you'll connect your calling in time, so it can share information with its past and future ways of being.

1.   Get your lab notebook.

2.   Go into your inner lab, and notice where you are as you enter the lab. Take a walk through your inner lab. Remember where you go (don't make your path too complicated). When you've visited most of your inner lab and you're ready to stand still for a bit, notice where you are at the end of the journey.

3. Now choose to stand in the very first location where you stood when you first arrived in your lab. In this "past" location, become your past self—just for now, you are representing the part of you that is still in that position, forever entering your inner lab. As this part of yourself, see how it feels to always be at the beginning of the path.

4. Now move to any location you visited during the middle part of your inner lab tour. Just for now, you are representing the present you, forever in the act of journeying around your inner lab. As this part of yourself, see how it feels to always be on the path.

5. Finally, move to the location where you ended the journey (end of step 2). Just for now, you are representing your future self, forever having already completed the journey. As this part of yourself, see how it feels to always be done.

6. Now walk backward and forward on your path. See how it feels to feel yourself representing the whole path—including all of your journey—all at once. This is what it feels like to connect you to your past and future selves in time.

7. Write down in your lab notebook any insights you've had in this process. Next, we'll connect your calling in time.

8. Split a page in your lab notebook into three columns, labeled Past, Present, and Future.

9. In the Present column, write down the inputs and outputs that you already connected in the previous exercise. If any other inputs or outputs come up, connect them in space (using the previous exercise) and then include these as well.

10. Imagine any point in your prior life when you were trying to engage your calling but it wasn't working. Representing that past version of your calling, write down in the Past column the inputs and outputs that are not connected there (in the past) but

that you wish had been connected at that time. Now imagine a point in your life when your calling is fully engaged in the world and you are in a state of joyful, easy flow. Representing that future version of your calling, write down in the Future column the inputs and outputs that you feel are fully connected in the future.

11. Now draw a circle around the Past, Present, and Future, and label the entire page "My evolving calling."

12. Use the full authority of your authentic self to love your evolving calling: past, present, and future.

It's interesting to shift your perspective to include your past, present, and future selves. But what creates sustainability is recognizing that, while your calling is evolving over time in its level of engagement and success in the world, all parts of that evolution can be present right now. This doesn't mean that right now you can force your calling to be what it will be in the future—actually, it's the opposite. By allowing your calling to be a success in the future, you are reducing the pressure on the present moment. You can see that your calling will get there, and you can even see how it will get there—by eventually connecting the appropriate inputs and outputs. But your calling doesn't need to be off in the future. In a way, there's a part of your successful true work that already lives, now.

To summarize, it may seem paradoxical, but by making the assumption that your calling has evolved from the past and will continue to evolve in its engagement with the world, you can let go of feeling that you need to get to full engagement of your calling right now. Instead, you can let full engagement of your calling do what it's supposed to do—literally *call you forward* toward it.

Letting your future call you forward means periodically seeing where your calling is going next and getting information about inputs and outputs you might need in the future. If that seems like a lot of work, don't worry. It's likely that, by the end of this program, you'll integrate this way of thinking into your daily life, so you may not need to explicitly redo the previous exercise each time you want to get some information or inspiration. But it is extremely helpful to give yourself permission to have this particular perspective shift, because when that permission is given, communication between past, present, and future versions of your true work becomes much more automatic. If you don't believe me, work your calling and see what happens by the end of this week.

Working Your Calling

Your calling is connected in time and space, and you're ready to engage it to work your calling. What does it mean to work your calling? In mechanical terms, it means to allow this process to turn the inputs into outputs. The mechanics of your calling will be unique to you, and you can use your user's guide as well as your current list of inputs and outputs to get clarity on those mechanics in an operational sense. But what does all that look like, practically, out in the world? It is different for each person, so you'll have to do an experiment to find out what it looks like for you. That's the last piece of work this week: the second Calling Experiment.

🔬 Calling Experiment 2

Goal: To engage your calling in the world while keeping it connected in space and time.

Time required: 1 to 2 hours

This experiment is similar to the one you did at the end of part I of this program, except instead of testing out your calling in the world, you're actually taking an action to engage your calling in the world, and you are recording the unique workings of your calling as you take that action. The whole thing won't take that long, but it will kick off the engagement of your calling in a healthy and sustainable way. It's time to watch your calling in action!

This experiment can seem complicated, so consider reading it all the way through before starting it.

1. Brainstorm.

    Get out your lab notebook, enter your inner laboratory, and brainstorm a list of actions that will practically engage your calling, given your current inputs and outputs. For example, imagine your calling is to be a voice for the unheard; your current inputs are news articles, requests for help, and time; and your current outputs are live performances and changes in state law. Your list might include taking time to check the news and your emails for requests for help, contacting congresspeople or running for office, writing a performance piece, or contacting a performance venue to plan a date for a performance. Include everything that comes up, including actions you think are very difficult or too easy. Include them all.

    When you sense that you're about done, look through the list and circle one action that is currently feeling very powerful and yet possible. All of these actions may need doing. You're just choosing one right now, with the full authority of your authentic self. That circled action is the action you'll commit to starting before the end of the week.

2. Plan your experiment.

    Now you have your action, but what about the experiment? The point of the experiment is to not only do the action but to learn how your calling works when it is engaged in the world. "How your calling works" is purposefully vague. It is up to you to decide what you are most interested in discovering about your calling's mechanics.

    Maybe you care about your calling's pace, the size of your steps, the immediacy of its impact on the world, all of these, or none of them. Take a moment in your inner lab and write down the questions you are interested in answering about how your calling works. Choose one of these questions and plan a simple experiment from your action, with the goal being to use your action to address your chosen question.

Keep your experiment very simple, something you could comfortably complete in an hour or so. Then in your lab notebook, write down a title for your experiment, a goal, a plan, and how you intend to interpret the results. Here's an example:

> **Experiment:** Start My Campaign for Office!
>
> **Goal:** To see how my calling needs to be paced when I am practically engaging it in the world.
>
> **Plan:** To draw a very rough outline for my campaign website while keeping in mind my inputs and outputs as well as the future versions of my calling.
>
> **Interpretation:** If I feel overwhelmed, I'll know I tried to do too much and I'll break off a smaller chunk for action in the future. If I feel in the flow and excited, and I want to keep going, I'll know that this is the pace suitable for my calling. If I feel bored, I'll know that I need to be more ambitious in my actions.

3. Get connected in time.

    Before doing your experiment, connect to your future self, who has completed the experiment. Did you do the right experiment? Does the experiment need to be tweaked in any way? Ask your future self these questions and trust your answers. Change your experiment if necessary.

4. Do your experiment before the end of the week.

    Observe yourself as you do your experiment, and be sure to record your results as well as your interpretation. Did you feel in the flow as you did your action? What did you learn? If you want to discover something new about how your calling works or you want to try another action, write another experiment, get connected in time, and do the new experiment.

Hopefully it's clear by now that you can create as many experiments as you want to help you understand the workings of your calling. This is your responsibility—no one else knows how your calling works. At the same time, it's also a source of freedom, in that your calling is free to work in exactly the way that it needs to. And no one else's rules about it will make a bit of difference. We have the responsibility to experiment and the freedom to interpret the results.

Conclusion

Welcome to your engaged calling! It's normal at this point to have mixed feelings. Maybe you're simultaneously thinking, "Wait, it's that easy?" and "It took a lot of work to get here!" Both are true—it takes a lot of hard work to get to a place where your calling can actually feel easy to engage. And as you complete this program, it'll get even easier.

There are only two weeks left. Next week, you'll work on surrendering the progress of your calling to the universe. Don't worry. It's less scary than it sounds, and it's a necessary last step to engaging your calling in the world. Then in the final week, you'll rework your calling user's manual, create a contract between your current and your fully engaged future calling, and celebrate everything you've done.

Experimenting with Surrender

Objective: To surrender the progress of your calling to the universe and appreciate the benevolence of the universe.

Why Surrender Is Necessary

Talking with people about surrendering almost always brings up resistance and fear. The word "surrender" itself comes from roots meaning "to give over." Most people assume that when you surrender you are unhealthily giving up something important, like your authority or power. This false assumption is what produces resistance and fear when people contemplate surrender. But there is such a thing as positive, healthy surrender, and this week is all about it.

It's not healthy to give away your own authority or power to someone else. So what does "positive surrender" mean? What would you be giving over to someone? And to whom, exactly, would you give this stuff? The answers are simple: you're giving over the progress of your calling, and you're surrendering this progress to the rest of the universe.

Why should you consider giving over the progress of your calling at all? Well, actually, you don't have to consider it. (Okay, you can contemplate it for hours on end if you want, but you don't actually have a say in surrendering.) This is one of those situations that is out of your control. Remember in Weeks 3 and 4 when you came to terms with your absolute authority only extending to your full authentic self, and your choices only being the best they can be at the time?

Well, your calling operates in the universe—not just in your full authentic self. When it comes to making your calling thrive in the universe, you absolutely need the rest of the universe outside of you to play along and do its part. And you don't have control over that. So surrendering the progress of your calling to the universe is actually necessary—because it's the only option if you want your calling to make progress.

But you do have some choices. You have to choose whether you want your calling to make progress, and you have to choose whether you can be sure of the universe's love for you and your calling. This week is about helping you make those choices.

Don't get this idea of surrender wrong—you still have the full authority of your authentic self, you still have trust, love, discernment, your user's manual, the Positivity Habit, your inputs and outputs...all of it. Everything you've learned so far is critical for your calling's progress.

The deal is that you can stop your calling's progress—you have absolute veto power over its success. You can do this by ignoring what you learned and carefully wrote about in your user's manual, by having a negative relationship with the rest of the universe, by not connecting your calling in space and time, or by allowing those space and time connections to fail. If you do any of these, you will stop the progress of your calling. So rest assured, you have ultimate power over stopping the progress of your calling.

Insight: You have absolute control over stopping the progress of your calling. All you have to do is undo the work you've already done and remember never to do it again.

If you've gotten this far in the program, chances are you don't need to shut things down permanently in this way. That doesn't mean there won't be times when you feel enough fear about your calling's progress that you do end up temporarily shutting down its progress to reorient yourself. That's normal and, in fact, it's a process that has a name. It's called the *dance of faith and fear*. It's a dance that will continue until you feel sure of the universe's benevolent intentions toward you and your calling.

Ellen: The Dance of Faith and Fear

Ellen*, a talented psychotherapist, told me about a healing she experienced. She was writing in her journal while she awaited knee surgery. As she wrote, she heard a commanding voice. It told her that her knees would be healed in that moment. She sat there, dumbfounded, not sure what to do. As she sat, her knees were healed. Ellen actually canceled her surgery, hopped on her bike, and rode around town. Inspiring!

But here's what happened the next day and the next: Ellen refused to write in her journal, afraid that doing so would somehow evoke this powerful voice. She was terrified by the power of her experience. When I asked her whether she thought she was schizophrenic, she said she didn't think so; she'd actually checked with her therapist. When I asked her if she thought it was the universe who spoke to her and healed her, she said yes. In that case, the experience must have reassured her that the universe is positive, something she can be in relationship with, right? "No!" she answered. She felt scared and didn't know why.

Ellen's story is a very dramatic version of what I call the dance of faith and fear. Here's how it happens. First, we start with something approaching faith: we believe the rest of the universe exists and can potentially be in a benevolent relationship with us. Initially, our desire to have proof of the benevolence of the universe gets us motivated. For Ellen, her beginner's faith is what made her able to hear that voice and receive her experience of healing. But when she had dramatic proof of an external universe that seemed to be benevolently interacting with her, Ellen moved over to fear. That's the dance. I have caught up with Ellen since that story—more miraculous things have happened to her, with a similar dancelike effect. However, each time something happens, she becomes more convinced that the universe holds her in a loving light.

When we are doing the dance of faith and fear, as soon as we get proof of the benevolence of the universe, we question our own side of the relationship. We may admit that the rest of the universe is benevolent, but we wonder if we're good enough (smart enough, powerful enough, strong enough, beautiful enough) to be in relationship with it. What if we are a disappointment to it? Our fear drives us back into faith, away from knowledge.

One way to stop swinging between faith and fear is to decide that the rest of the universe is indifferent to us. The universe is just out there, grooving along without us. It doesn't need us. This way, we don't even get into faith, and we can avoid having any fear at all—or so we think. Actually, this method leads to even stronger fear, since we can end up feeling so alone.

The frightening truth is that the universe is in relationship with us already, and we with it. In Week 9 we worked to make this relationship positive, but positivity is not the same as acknowledging actual benevolence—actual love coming your way from the rest of the universe. Benevolence implies that you can rely on the universe to support you in your calling's progress.

The first step to true surrender is to leave this beginner's faith behind and accept love from the rest of the universe. This will allow you to choose whether you can be sure of the universe's love for you and your calling. Faith is really reserved for things you are not sure of. You don't have faith in your shoes, for instance. You know they are there and that they will do their job.

We do need faith when we are unsure—we need our desire to know the nature of the universe's intentions toward us to get us moving toward actual firm knowledge. Yet once we are sure of these intentions, we have to let go of beginner's faith. After all, do your relationships flourish when you are stuck wondering whether someone else loves you?

Insight: The first step to surrendering is to accept love from the rest of the universe.

When you're in the dance of faith and fear, you don't have to acknowledge and appreciate this love. You can wonder about whether it exists, whether you're good enough for it, or both. You can do that forever—but if you choose to engage your calling in the world, you need to leave this dance. You need to become sure of the benevolent nature of the universe in relationship to you and your calling. This brief exercise will help you begin to leave the dance of faith and fear behind.

Brief Exercise

This activity is about listening to what the rest of the universe has to say to you.

1. Get your lab notebook and set it aside. Set a timer for five minutes. Go into your inner lab. Tell the universe that you plan to listen for the next five minutes and that you are open to whatever you hear, as long as it is kind. Commit to noticing any feelings, sensations, images, or words that come up. For example, if you feel strange planning to listen to the universe, say to yourself, "Yes, I feel strange planning to listen to the universe," and then move on to step 2.

2. Until the timer goes off, be quiet and pay attention to anything you sense. Let yourself just listen without talking back. The universe is most likely to speak in a quiet voice or not through words at all. You may just have a sense of love surrounding you, or you might feel an urge to do something specific. Forgive yourself whenever you notice yourself drift off, then return to listening.

3. After you are done listening, write in your lab notebook about what you experienced. Include your sense of what the universe was like—how did it feel when it was relating to you? Let yourself record exactly your experience, even if it was odd or surprising.

This is an exercise to turn to whenever you wonder whether the universe has loving intentions toward you. You may feel that you're making up whatever you experience—that's fine. Your experience of the universe's sentiments toward you will only ever come through the same faculty you use to access intuition: your superconscious. Regardless of that fact, these sentiments matter a great deal. Because once you understand that you are loved by the universe, you can get major practical support for your calling.

Asking for Support

When you ask the rest of the universe for support, you partner with it. You are assuming that its relationship with you is positive, that it loves you, and that you are worthy of working with the rest of the universe. Instead of being a supplicant, you become a partner. You transcend the dance of faith and fear, and you make the choice to allow your true work to thrive.

But a word to the wise: asking the universe for support creates this essential partnership by asking for something of you in return. What it asks of you is that you don't sabotage your own request. Asking the universe for help in engaging your calling can be a frightening thing to do. If you receive what you ask for, you have to do the work that follows. If you don't receive what you've asked for, you might fear that it's because you don't deserve the help after all—sending you back into the dance of faith and fear. To avoid facing these fears, you might sabotage any assistance the universe can offer. The most common form of sabotage is to ask for support without the full authority of your authentic self, so it doesn't feel too bad if later you don't receive it.

If you ask for help with the full authority of your authentic self, you aren't holding a piece of yourself back. You are admitting that every part of you wants what you are asking for—which means that you risk becoming hurt and angry if you don't get it.

Insight: The second step to true surrender is to ask for help from the universe without sabotaging your own request.

When I was a personal coach, I met a group of other coaches in the Chicago area. Denene, one of the most impressive, told me about her plan to travel to a conference she wanted to attend. She couldn't afford the plane fare, so her idea was to call the president of United Airlines and ask for a round-trip ticket at a deep discount. I couldn't believe it. I was scared for her; I told her that she should be prepared to be laughed at or to not even reach the president at all. By saying this to her, I was trying to get her to adopt my own fear that she would be disappointed. To my surprise, Denene light-heartedly laughed and said she would just go for it. I felt sorry for her and hoped for the best.

She called me back the next day and told me what had happened. She had reached the president after all. And he had given her the ticket. Round-trip! He also asked her to provide his employees with some coaching on how to put themselves on the line as powerfully as she had. Meanwhile, I had been discouraging Denene with my fear, which could have led her to sabotage her own request! Luckily, she had asked with her whole self and not listened to my well-meaning but wrongheaded attitude.

Asking, like faith, is an in-between state. You want help that you don't currently have, so you use the bridge of asking. The challenge is being able to ask with your whole self, then move to the other side of the bridge and see whether you receive what you've asked for. You may or may not receive it, and that's a risk you need to openly and full-heartedly take with your whole self, without sabotaging the experiment. The Asking Experiment will help you see how that feels while simultaneously supporting your calling in thriving in the world.

⚗ The Asking Experiment

Goal: With your whole self, to openly ask the universe to help your calling thrive.

Time required: 30 minutes

This is the last experiment in the program, and it's one that you'll do whenever your calling needs extra support. To receive the help that the universe can offer you—to partner in your calling so that your calling can succeed and thrive—is one of the greatest pleasures of life. Ask early, before you're desperate for help. Ask often, whenever you feel like being reminded of the love the universe has for you.

1.   Define your requests.

     Go into your inner lab and bring your lab notebook. Make ten requests of the universe that you feel would support your calling. Write these down and include today's date. Dare yourself to ask for help in areas that you feel might be near impossible, such as contact with a leader in the targeted field, an email from a potential funder, a positive response from a mentor, clarity about how to integrate your current job with your calling.

2.   Fine-tune your requests.

     Stay open to what you really choose. Spend some time opening up your requests a bit more broadly—general is good, in case you don't know exactly the right thing for your calling. For example, if you think you want to win the lottery, explore whether money or success is your true desire. Having said that, be true to your desire: Don't ask for a chance to play any instrument at a local bar when what you really want is to play keyboards at Carnegie Hall. If that's the only course of action that you choose with all of yourself, ask to have a chance to play keyboards at Carnegie Hall.

Notice if you close yourself off to something because you fear you won't get it—this is sabotaging your request. If you find yourself doing this, refer to your user's guide and do whatever practice or exercise helps you move through fear. Finalize your list of requests in your lab notebook.

3. Ask with your whole self.

    Talk about, pray, or meditate on what you've asked for every day for a week. As you ask, concentrate on the way the universe feels to you, not how you think the universe should feel intellectually. Make it a personal relationship, not a conceptual one. Notice if you feel at home in your inner lab—staying right in your authority and your authenticity as you ask. If you aren't feeling at home, perhaps consult your user's guide for how to deal with feeling inauthentic or not in touch with your authority. If you find that you need to adjust what you are asking for, that's fine. Just edit down your list of requests.

4. Listen with the full authority of your authentic self.

    Each day, after you talk, pray, or meditate, ask the universe what you need to do in this partnership, if anything. Then listen and write down what you sense or hear. Each day, mark a request as received if you've already received it.

5. Record the results.

    At the end of the week, look through your list of requests and record what you did and didn't receive, if that's not clear already. Record how you feel about receiving and not receiving your requests. If you feel mad, relieved, excited, afraid, overjoyed, or confused at the universe, write it down. Your feelings are the keys to uncovering how it feels to work with the universe.

What if you don't get what you've asked for? Then you could decide that the universe does not love you or that you are not worthy. That would mean you would enter the dance of faith and fear again, staying out of relationship with the universe.

But here's another possibility: you might recognize that receiving what you ask for is only one possible outcome of this experiment, and it's really not the point. The real result of this experiment is that you will be aware of the love the universe has for you.

You already have beliefs and opinions about how the universe should behave. You have feelings about any slights or surprises the universe slips you, and you are joyful when you can feel the universe loving you. These are all feelings that happen in a relationship. This experiment teaches that you already have a loving relationship with the universe; you are already sure of the universe's love. The truth is in your experience. Here you are, receiving love from the universe and allowing your calling to progress. Nice choice!

Roselyn: The Power of Surrender

Perhaps the best way to end this week is to tell the story of Roselyn, who knows about surrender from events in her life as well as her work. Roselyn is a psychiatrist in her thirties who specializes in working with adolescents. She was raised in a religious household and, as an adult, has a strong and deeply examined spiritual life.

I asked her about her earliest glimpse of her calling, and she told me about being fourteen and at the hospital when her mother was dying from a brain tumor. "It was an overwhelming experience—being there with my family, being asked to make life support decisions. But there was a candy striper teen, a volunteer who kept trying to offer us water. I can't put words to my feelings at the moment she offered the water. It made such an impression on me. The possibility of helping others opened up to me in a way that hadn't been there before. I could see that what she was doing did not solve the problem of my mother dying in any way, she was just trying to offer something in the face of what couldn't be fixed. I don't think we took any of her water, and she was probably almost as bewildered as we were. But to have someone be in that space and also be bewildered and vulnerable and wanting to help—that made an impression."

I asked Roselyn to define her calling now, and she said, "I'm a healer, but that's a misnomer. When people do heal, they heal themselves or are healed beyond human efforts, by something beyond themselves. A lot of the wounds I see are not healable in the same way as a physical wound. They're something that has to be borne not healed. Like my mother's tumor and her death as well. I guess I am compelled to heal the unhealable. In a way, I'm a minister, and I think all doctors are—to the extent they accept that, it makes them effective."

To this point, Roselyn told me that she once worked with a family doctor during her training. She went with him to see a child who had just fallen on the playground; his mom had brought him in. They prepared to examine the child, but they already knew from the nurse's information that he was fine. The doctor looked at her and said, "We'll just—" and then he made the sign of the cross. Roselyn understood. "We were treating the fear in the mother that the kid was not okay. We could have been frustrated with them taking our time. But that doctor taught me that there was a sacramental role in what we did, set apart from the every day. We're engaging in rituals of healing, and they work. I think we would do well to learn from the better ministers of different faith traditions— the best ones don't have too high an opinion of what they themselves can accomplish. These are people who see themselves more as a vessel or a messenger of something bigger. Not in a way that makes them better or special but because it's their role, their calling. A calling is not a superpower."

Her recognition that a calling is not a superpower comes directly from Roselyn's deep experience with surrendering. She knows she is not infallible and that she cannot heal everyone.

She also knows that, at times, she needs healing. Perhaps paradoxically, that may be what makes Roselyn an effective healer. That, and the sense of humor that inevitably comes with surrendering to the universe. When I asked Roselyn what advice she would give to her fourteen-year-old self at her mother's hospital bedside, given what she has learned so far, she laughed and said, "I'd tell her, 'Take the water!'"

Conclusion

You've danced with faith and fear, you've listened to the universe, and you've even let the universe support you this week. No matter your experience of the Asking Experiment, you learned about staying in relationship with the universe. You even felt a taste of what it would be like to surrender to the universe and allow it to move and shape your calling for you.

You're almost there. This program is winding down, and your calling is setting sail. Next week you'll ask yourself some essential questions about your calling, so you can see your calling with a new perspective. And you'll conclude the program with a brief but important celebration of all you've done. But the fun is just beginning. After this program is complete, you'll have the rest of your life to discover how your calling evolves.

Your Life, Your Calling

Objective: To get perspective on your calling and celebrate completing this program.

Part of the Whole

When I was in graduate school, I somehow convinced my dissertation adviser to send me to a neuroscience conference in Schiermonnikoog. This is a small, fog-blanketed island in the Netherlands. It is a perfect place to think heady thoughts about how the brain might work.

During one of the breaks from the conference, I rented a bike for two dollars and rode around the island. As I rode, I noticed a field of grass gone to seed, and above it I saw a circle of gulls. The circle really impressed me. Though it's a common sight for coast dwellers, this circling was unusually beautiful to my Midwestern eyes. I rode off the trail to the middle of the field so I could see the gulls more clearly. When I was close enough to the seagulls' circle, I hopped off my bike to lie in the grass and stare up at the birds. Looking carefully, I could see the path that each bird created, and my truth reaction coursed through me when I realized that none of the birds was actually flying in a circle.

One bird did an arc about a quarter of the length around the circle, while another flew up and down, defining the edge of the circle. Another gull flew about a half of the circle then returned by retracing its path. But not a single seagull flew the entire circle, even though as a whole their circle was so clear I could trace it in the sky. The experience shook me. I heard myself whisper, "I thought I had to do the whole circle," and I felt tears pressing against my eyes.

Insight: Your calling is big, but it is also only a part of the whole.

Years later, a friend of mine studying theology casually mentioned to me that one thing she thought was cool about Islam is the idea that we are all holding part of a universal wheel. No one has the whole wheel, but we each have a part. Our only job is to turn our part. Of course, we wonder about the plan for the universe and how it will all work out when it can seem so weird and painful and crazy. Even so, our job is to keep turning our part of the wheel. It means transcending ourselves.

As mentioned in the introduction to this book, *self-transcendence* means allowing your gifts to be used in the service of something larger than yourself. In his address on receiving the Philadelphia Liberty Medal, Vaclav Havel (1994) summarized the importance of self-transcendence:

> ...In today's multicultural world, the truly reliable path to peaceful coexistence and creative cooperation must start from what is at the root of all cultures and what lies infinitely deeper in human hearts and minds than political opinion, convictions, antipathies, or sympathies: it must be rooted in self-transcendence.

There is an essential balance between the needs of the part and the needs of the whole, and this program has worked to teach you that balance. It's like this: When your needs are met, you can pursue your calling. When you pursue your calling, you can support others in their callings. Once everyone is pursuing their callings, the universe's needs are met.

It's time to place your calling in perspective, so you can see how your piece fits in the universal puzzle, how it fit even before you knew what it was, and how it might evolve in the future.

The Five Questions

I've asked hundreds of people about their true work. Many people have told me that these conversations are clarifying for them. Over time, I've learned that five questions are particularly useful to help gain perspective on your true work. This week, you'll ask these questions of yourself. Now that you've come this far, your answers will come easily—but you may yet have some surprises in store.

Brief Exercise

Let's go through the five questions now and discover what they reveal.

1. Get out your lab notebook and enter your inner lab. Remember the full authority of your authentic self and access trust, discernment, and love.

2. Write down the following questions and answer each of them in turn:

    *   In my own words, what does a "calling" or "true work" mean?

    *   What is the earliest glimmer I can remember that relates to my own true work?

    *   How do I define my calling now?

    *   What have I done in the past and what can I do in the future if I lose faith in my true work?

    *   What would I say or do, knowing what I know now, if I could visit myself during the time when I had the earliest glimmer of my calling?

3. When done, write down any insights or perspectives you gained about your true work.

Your calling existed before you knew what it was, and it will continue to exist into the future. That doesn't mean it won't evolve—it will. It will morph and shift along with you as you grow. It's time to celebrate everything you've done and the remarkable future of your calling yet to unfold.

An Evolving Calling

Remember when I talked about my own experience of becoming a mother, when I realized I was dealing with splintered paths? One was the "mommy path" and the other was the "scientist path"? Well, I united those paths into a single, unitary path. But just a few days prior to completing the final manuscript for this book, that single path changed, in a healthy way. I attended my son's high school graduation. I don't love the multihour ceremonies and speeches of graduations, especially not in the hot sun. But as soon as I saw my son marching and I heard the first bars of "Pomp and Circumstance," I was in tears. I shouted, "I see you! You're my boy!" and immediately hoped he didn't hear me, because that would have embarrassed him terribly.

I was crying from joy as well as sadness. I was so proud of my son, but I was also in grief. I felt the "mommy" part of my unitary path retreating, out of necessity. My work now, I knew, was to be a scientist first and a mother second—and in so doing, to leave space for him to bring his own calling into the world. My path has evolved, and I know my calling will evolve in response to the new stretch of road.

Your calling can also evolve independently from other people. Further realizations and insights may come to you that expand or contract your definition of your calling, and life events may happen to you that appear to completely redefine your true work.

I say "appear to" because, if you've carefully done the work in this program, it would be unusual for your currently well-defined calling to be unrelated to an evolved understanding of your true work. Usually the thread connecting your present and future calling will be apparent, and when the time comes to examine your calling in detail again, you'll find that recognizing this thread of commonality will help you further understand who you are and what you're doing here.

> **Insight:** Your true work—your soul's work—is now well understood. The details may evolve, elements of your calling may come and go, but you don't have to seek anymore.

It can be addictive to work on yourself, to always try to gain a better understanding. You can worry that you aren't doing everything perfectly, that you still don't know exactly what to do yet. If you're feeling this way, remember that your true work is a process. Hook up your inputs and outputs in space and time, and watch your calling go.

Another way is to feel complete, for now, and celebrate your completeness. See if you can try this. Why? Because celebration will allow you to move into action and evolution.

Brief Exercise

It's time to tell your story and have a party!

1. Contact at least one person in your calling circle and ask them to celebrate your completion of the Calling program with you. This celebration can be anything: going for a walk, blowing out candles on a cake, or hosting a party for fifty people. Choose what would make you feel best and plan that.

2. At your celebration, consider telling the story of your calling. What was it like for you to go through this program? What did

you learn? What was it like before you started? What were you scared of? How did you move past those fears? What do you think comes next for you? How will you pursue your calling in the days, weeks, months, and years ahead? If you feel like keeping all of this private, that's fine too. Just celebrate, and make sure that the people at the celebration support you and your calling.

3. After the celebration is over, write in your lab notebook your thoughts and feelings about the experience of marking the completion of your Calling program—and the beginning of the rest of your life.

Celebrations are almost always bittersweet—they mark endings and beginnings. The flow of time keeps pulling our lives forward, and this won't change, even when you are sure about how to proceed to pursue your calling. What's different now is that you don't have to wonder what you're doing or how to do it; you know. And now you can simply do it, along with the entire universe.

Conclusion

It may seem that you're on your own now, but you're not on your own at all. You have your authentic self, your calling circle, http://www.thecallingprogram.com, and the entire rest of the universe for support, trust, and love.

Rabbi Zusya of Hanipoli once said, "When I die, God will not ask me, 'Why weren't you more like Moses?' God will ask me, 'Why weren't you more like Zusya?'"

The rest of the world needs your calling to shine so we can see the glory of the universe. This is how important you are. Thank you for giving your true self, and all its varied and delicious fruits, to the world.

Acknowledgments

Big thank you to my calling circle: Sue, Carol, Betty, and Diane, as well as everyone who offered feedback about the YouTube videos and *Unfolding*. Much gratitude to my remarkable editors, Vicraj Gill, Jennye Garibaldi, and Marisa Solís, who valiantly made this program into what it could be, and to the marketing and publicity team at New Harbinger. And to Camille Hayes, who approached me about writing this book several years ago. Also thanks to my friends and colleagues who provided interviews that greatly enriched the program. Finally, I am grateful to my family, especially Brooks and Joseph, who support my calling every day.

References

Assagioli, R. 1965. *Psychosynthesis: A Manual of Principles and Techniques*. New York: Penguin.

Baylor, A. L. 1997. A Three-Component Conception of Intuition: Immediacy, Sensing Relationships, and Reason. *New Ideas in Psychology* 15 (2): 185–194.

Bechara, A., H. Damasio, D. Tranel, and A. R. Damasio. 2005. "The Iowa Gambling Task and the Somatic Marker Hypothesis: Some Questions and Answers." *Trends in Cognitive Sciences* 9: 159–162.

National Scientific Council on the Developing Child. 2015. *Supportive Relationships and Active Skill-Building Strengthen the Foundations of Resilience: Working Paper No. 13*. Center on the Developing Child at Harvard University. Retrieved from http://www.developingchild.harvard.edu.

Crabtree, A. 2017. *Evolutionary Love and the Ravages of Greed*. Victoria, BC: Friesen Press.

Csikszentmihalyi, M. 1993. *The Evolving Self: A Psychology for the Third Millennium* (vol. 5). New York: HarperCollins.

DePaulo, B. M., and W. L. Morris. 2004. "Discerning Lies from Truths: Behavioural Cues to Deception and the Indirect Pathway of Intuition." In *The Detection of Deception in Forensic Contexts*, edited by Pär Anders Granhag and Leif A. Strömwall. Cambridge: Cambridge University Press.

Dijksterhuis, A., M. W. Bos, L. F. Nordgren, and R. B. Van Baaren. 2006. "On Making the Right Choice: The Deliberation-Without-Attention Effect." *Science* 311: 1,005–1,007.

Frank, M. G., P. Ekman, and W. V. Friesen. 1993. "Behavioral Markers and Recognizability of the Smile of Enjoyment." *Journal of Personality and Social Psychology* 64: 83–93.

Hannah, S. T., F. O. Walumbwa, and L. W. Fry. 2011. "Leadership in Action Teams: Team Leader and Members' Authenticity, Authenticity Strength, and Team Outcomes." *Personnel Psychology* 64: 771–802.

Hassin, R. 2013. "Yes It Can: On the Functional Abilities of the Human Unconscious." *Perspectives on Psychological Science* 8: 195–207.

Havel, V. 1994. "The Need for Transcendence in a Postmodern World." Speech given at Independence Hall, Philadelphia, PA.

Holden, L. M. 2005. "Complex Adaptive Systems: Concept Analysis." *Journal of Advanced Nursing* 52 (6): 651–657.

Kaplan, F., and P. Y. Oudeyer. 2004. "Maximizing Learning Progress: An Internal Reward System for Development." In *Embodied Artificial Intelligence*. Springer, Berlin: Heidelberg.

Kernis, M. H. 2003. "Toward a Conceptualization of Optimal Self-Esteem." *Psychological Inquiry* 14: 1–26.

Koltko-Rivera, M. E. 2006. "Rediscovering the Later Version of Maslow's Hierarchy of Needs: Self-Transcendence and Opportunities for Theory, Research, and Unification." *Review of General Psychology* 10: 302–317.

Kross, E., and O. Ayduk. 2011. "Making Meaning out of Negative Experiences by Self-Distancing." *Current Directions in Psychological Science* 20: 187–191.

Mischel, W. 2014. *The Marshmallow Test: Understanding Self-Control and How to Master it*. New York: Random House.

Mossbridge, J. A., and D. Radin. 2018a. "Precognition as a Form of Prospection: A Review of the Evidence." *Psychology of Consciousness: Theory, Research, and Practice* 5 (1): 78–93.

Mossbridge, J. A., and D. Radin. 2018b. "Plausibility, Statistical Interpretations and a New Outlook: Response to Commentaries on a Precognition Review." *Psychology of Consciousness: Theory, Research, and Practice* 5 (1): 110–116.

Politico. 2017. "Townsend: Trump Team Approached Me for FBI Director.", *Women Rule* podcast. Accessed September 18, 2017. http://www.politico.com/story/2017/05/24/townsend-trump-team-approached-me-for-fbi-director-238731.

Surakka, V., and J. K. Hietanen. 1998. "Facial and Emotional Reactions to Duchenne and Non-Duchenne Smiles." *International Journal of Psychophysiology* 29: 23–33.

Walumbwa, F. O., B. J. Avolio, W. L. Gardner, T. S. Wernsing, and S. J. Peterson. 2008. "Authentic Leadership: Development and Validation of a Theory-Based Measure." *Journal of Management* 34: 89–126.

Julia Mossbridge, PhD, is a visiting scholar at Northwestern University, fellow at the Institute of Noetic Sciences, science director at Focus@Will Labs, and associated professor of integral and transpersonal psychology at the California Institute of Integral Studies. Her research primarily involves understanding how time is perceived by our unconscious and conscious minds, and is secondarily related to authenticity and human interconnectivity. Mossbridge has a doctorate in communication sciences and disorders from Northwestern University, and a master's degree in neuroscience from the University of California, San Francisco. The 2014 winner of the Charles Honorton Integrative Contributions Award, she is coauthor (with Imants Barušs) of *Transcendent Mind*, author of *The Garden* and *Unfolding*, as well as coauthor of *The Premonition Code* in addition to multiple scientific articles. She is also inventor of Choice Compass, a patented physiologically based decision-making app.

Foreword writer **Carole Griggs, PhD**, is an executive coach, leadership development consultant, university professor, international speaker, researcher, author, and developer of transformative technology tools focused on human potential and consciousness evolution.

MORE BOOKS for the SPIRITUAL SEEKER

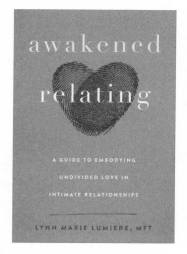

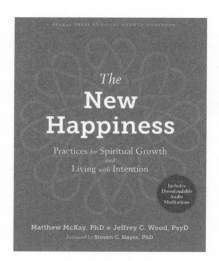
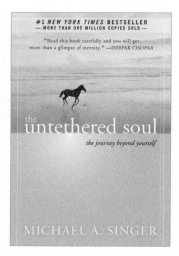